Twenty-seven Books in Thirteen Weeks

A Survey of the New Testament

Sue Crabtree

ISBN: 978-0-89098-921-0

©2017 by 21st Century Christian

2809 12th Ave S, Nashville, TN 37204

All rights reserved.

Cover design by Jonathan Edelhuber

Table of Contents

Preface

Often in Bible study, adults spend time on one book or one era of time and don't get the whole picture. This book is written to give a frame for New Testament study. There are three areas of study in the New Testament: The Life of Christ, The History of the Church in Acts, The Epistles and Revelation. I hope this book will be used in Bible classes and also in homes to encourage people to study the Bible more in depth.

This study can be completed in thirteen weeks, twenty-six weeks or it could be studied for an entire year. There are many activities and suggestions for class participation and a section on how to teach this material.

I am indebted to many great teachers who led me in this study. Many of the ideas presented here were gleaned from others. Special thanks to Sibyl Garrett for proofreading the book.

May we have a strong desire to grasp knowledge, attitudes, and skills from a study of the New Testament.

Sue Crabtree

Format of the Lessons

Fact Sheets   Outlines, information, character lists, and map searches.

Questions   Short answer, matching, and thought questions are provided.

Application   An application lesson with assignments and an action guide for each week are provided.

Special Challenges   Each chapter has several special challenges for the students. These can be selected by the student, assigned, or done in class.

Suggestions   Several suggestions are made about how to teach the lessons.

Sharing and praying are suggested. There are several options for teaching.

Answers   Answers to the short-answer and final exam questions are in the back.

Twenty-seven Books in Thirteen Weeks

We are starting a new adventure,
From the Old Testament to the New.
Come along and join us,
You'll find God's Word is true.

Grab your Bible and the handbook,
And let's be on our way,
With a good Christian teacher,
We'll not be led astray.

Within the four great gospels,
See the sacrifice of Christ.
In the Acts of the Apostles,
The church will come to life.

Then on to the epistles,
Written by some inspired men.
Learn more about salvation,
And how to conquer sin.

The last is Revelation
And then the journey's done.
Our faith will be made stronger
In the light of God's own son.

Sue Mitchell

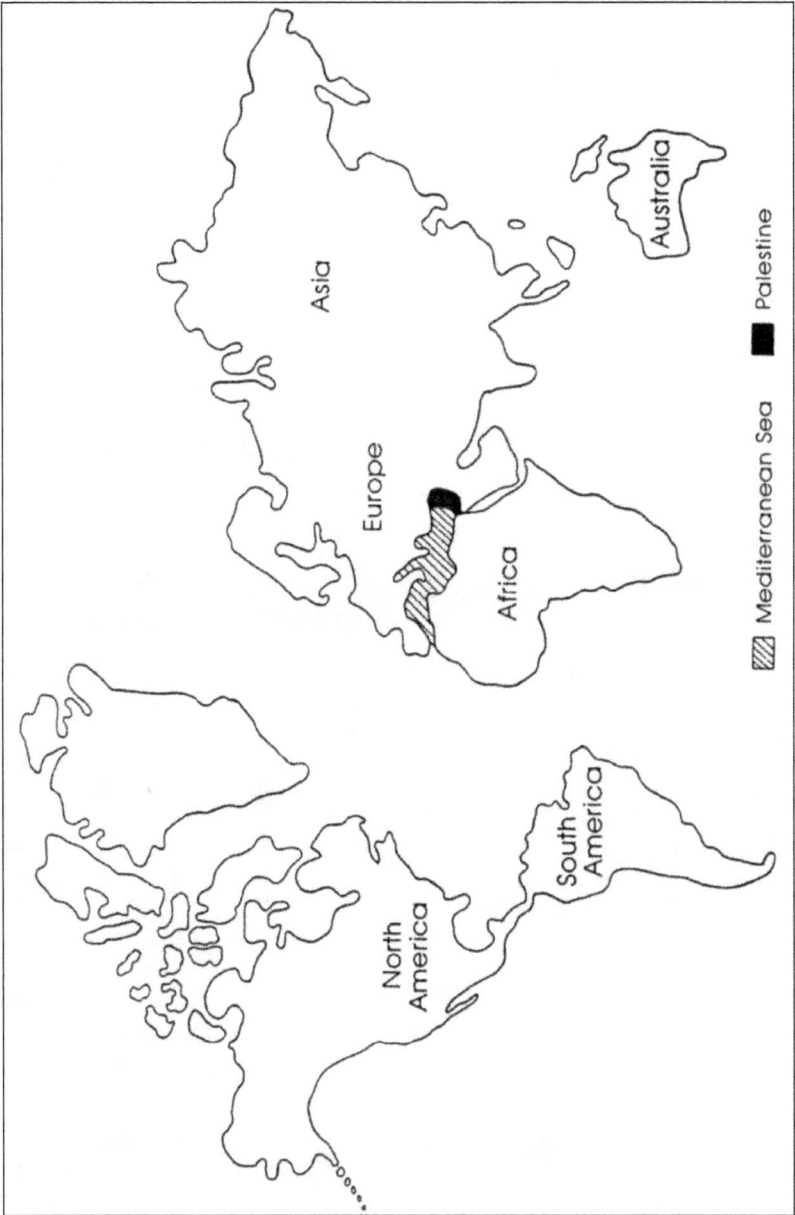

Asia

Australia

Europe

Africa

North America

South America

▨ Mediterranean Sea   ■ Palestine

May be reproduced for classroom use.

PHOENICIA

BASHAN

Mediterranean Sea

GALILEE

Sea of
Galilee

DECAPOLIS

SAMARIA

PEREA

JUDEA

Dead Sea

**Provinces
of Palestine**

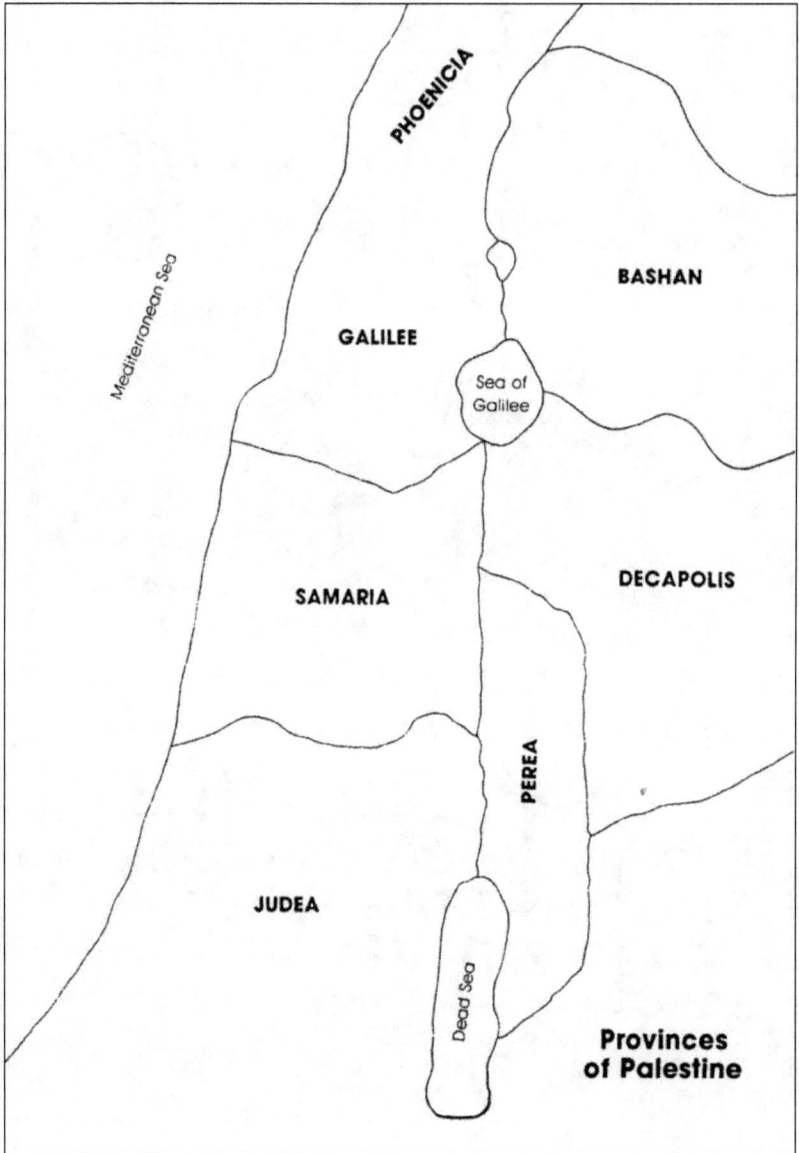

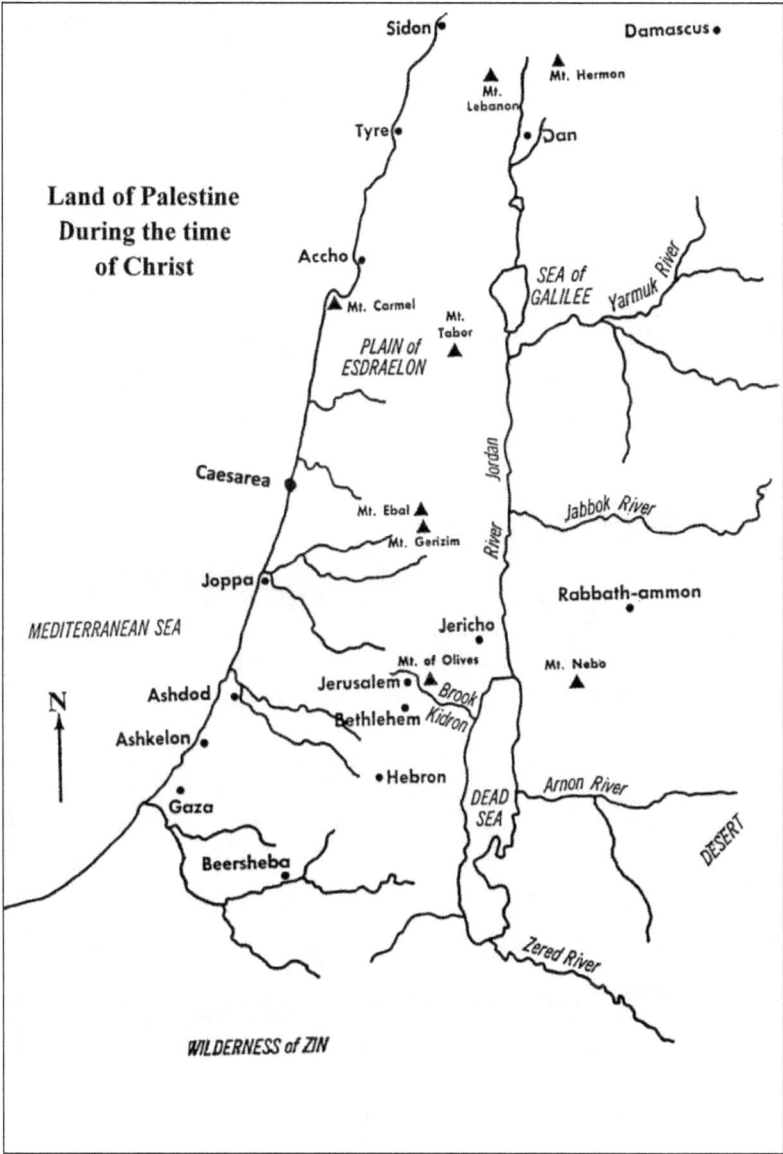

Land of Palestine
During the time
of Christ

Sidon

Damascus

Mt. Hermon

Mt. Lebanon

Tyre

Dan

Accho

SEA of GALILEE

Yarmuk River

Mt. Carmel

Mt. Tabor

PLAIN of ESDRAELON

Caesarea

Jordan River

Jabbok River

Mt. Ebal

Mt. Gerizim

Joppa

MEDITERRANEAN SEA

Rabbath-ammon

Jericho

Mt. of Olives

Jerusalem

Mt. Nebo

N

Ashdod

Bethlehem

Brook Kidron

Ashkelon

Hebron

Gaza

DEAD SEA

Arnon River

DESERT

Beersheba

Zered River

WILDERNESS of ZIN

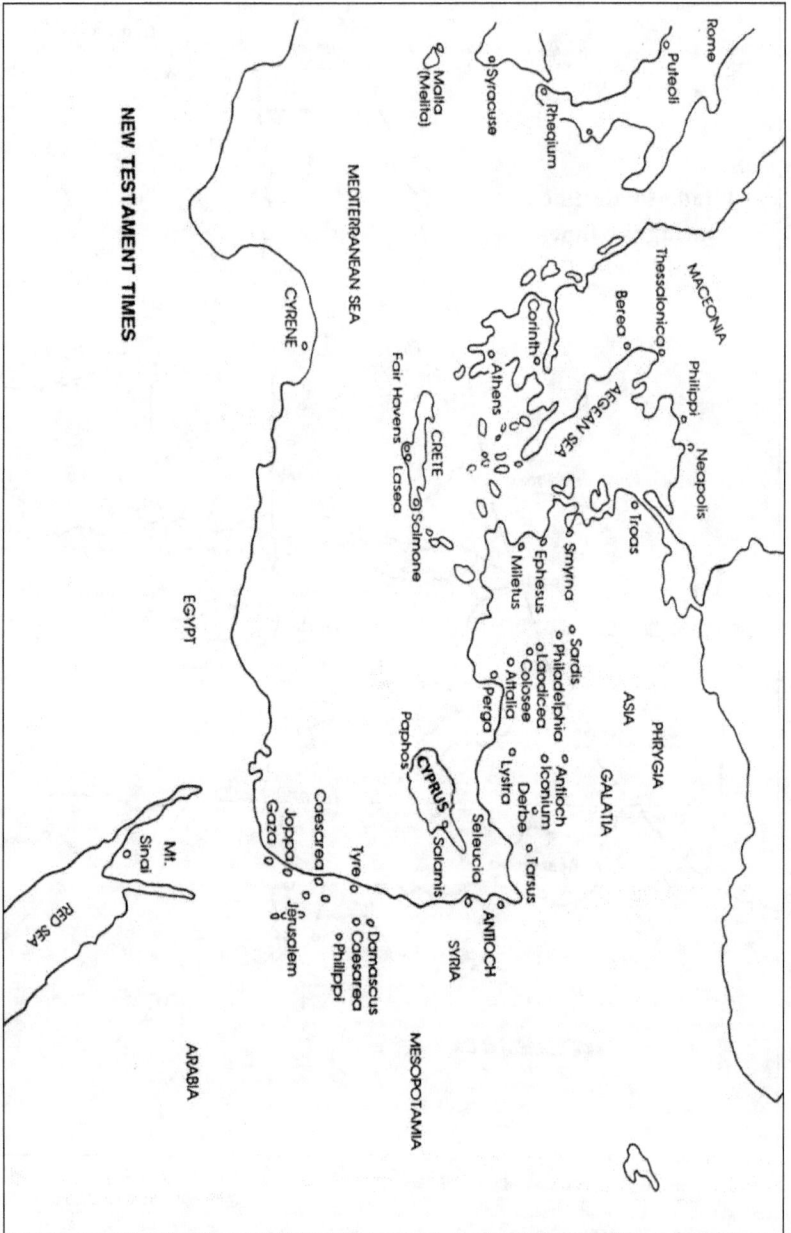

NEW TESTAMENT TIMES

Chapter One

Introduction to the New Testament

Fact Sheet

Number of Books: There are 39 books in the Old Testament and 27 books in the New Testament. To remember this, count the letters in *Old* and you will get 3. Then count the letters in *Testament*, and you will get 9. Put the numbers together, and you will get 39, the number of books in the Old Testament. Now multiply 3 x 9 = 27, the number of books in the New Testament.

Eras or Ages of Time: God has dealt with His people during three different ages of time. There were the Patriarchal, Mosaical, and Christian ages. The Patriarchal period (2,500 years) is told in the book of Genesis in the Old Testament, and God talked directly with the Fathers during this time. During the Mosaical Period (1,500 years), God gave them a law and He spoke to the people through the prophets. During the Christian Age, which began with the death of Christ, God speaks through Jesus and the Word.

Between the Testaments: There were 400 years between the Old Testament and the New Testament. During this time, the Greeks conquered Palestine; and then the Romans came into power. The Old Testament was translated into Greek (the universal language), and Romans built roads, which paved the way for Christianity. Synagogues were places of worship; and Pharisees, Sadducees, and Herodians were some of the sects of the Jews. There were many changes during the 400 years of the period between the testaments.

Categories of the Books: Matthew, Mark, Luke, and John are Gospels about the life of Christ. Acts is a history of the church. There are 21 books or epistles about Christian living, and one book of prophecy, Revelation.

Writers of the New Testament: There are eight writers of the New

Testament. **Matthew** wrote Matthew. **Mark** wrote Mark. **Luke** wrote Luke and Acts, and **John** wrote five books: Gospel of John; 1,2,3 John, and Revelation, **Peter** wrote 1,2 Peter. **James** wrote James. **Jude** wrote Jude. **Paul** wrote 13 books. Biblical scholars aren't sure who wrote Hebrews.

The Gospel Writers: Matthew wrote to the Jews, and because of this, he presented Jesus as a king. Mark wrote to Romans who were mighty and powerful, so he presented Jesus as a servant. Luke wrote to Greeks who were interested in intellect, so he presented Jesus as a man. John wrote to Christians, so he presented Jesus as God. It is important to remember this as we study.

Distinctives of the Books: Scholars do not agree about the date of the books, but all usually agree that John was the last Gospel written.

Only about 7 percent of the book of Matthew is distinctive to Matthew; about 42 percent of Mark is distinctive to Mark; and about 59 percent of Luke is distinctive to Luke. Eighty percent of what is in John is not in the other books.

Differences Among the Groups: The Jews put emphasis on their past and their religion. They observed the commands from God. The Greeks put emphasis on wisdom and the future. They were bound to their culture. The Romans put emphasis on the present and the commands of Caesar, and they were busy with construction. The Christians put emphasis on God's Word and Christ and were looking forward to heaven.

Languages: The Old Testament was written mostly in Hebrew, and the New Testament was written mostly in Greek. When the Bible was translated into Greek, it became available for all readers of that day.

Character List: Writers of the New Testament (listed in this chapter)

Application: How do we know that the Bible is the Word of God? There are usually three ways you can tell. The Bible does not conflict with science. For example, the Bible says the world is round and hangs suspended on nothing (Isaiah 40:22, Job 26:7). Science bears this out. Second, there are so many prophecies that have been fulfilled where the prophets could not have known what would happen without God's hand. Third, the Bible was written over a period of 1,400 years by 40 different men who were scattered all over the face of the earth, yet they all told the same story of redemption and the grace of God. There have not been any proven contradictions. How could they have done this?

Second Timothy 3:16-17 says that God breathed or inspired the Word of God. Second Peter 1:21 says, "For prophecy never had its origin in the will of man, but men spoke from God as they were carried along by the Holy Spirit."

Because the Bible comes from God, we must love and respect it. Read one of David's psalms to see how much he loved God's Word (Psalms 150).

Do we love God's Word? Does this encourage us to study the Bible?

Assignment: Learn to write and spell the books of the New Testament this week.

Set a new goal about Bible study:

• daily Bible reading
• taking a class at a Christian school
• teaching someone about the Bible
• studying in depth a certain book.

Action Guide: Write a poem about the Bible and the importance of it in your life or choose one of the challenges on page 13. The poem you write doesn't have to rhyme.

Short-Answer Questions

1. Which gospel writers tell of the birth of Christ?
2. Which gospel writers tell of the death of Christ?
3. Why did one writer tell one story and another writer tell another story?
4. Which gospel writer includes no parables?
5. Who was the only writer to tell of the raising of Lazarus from the dead?
6. Explain how God dealt with His people during the three eras of time?
7. How can we be sure the Bible came from God?
8. Which gospel was written last?

9. Name the writers of the New Testament.

10. Name some of the events during the period between the testaments.

11. In what language was the New Testament written?

Thought Questions

1. How much of the Bible do we have to know to be saved?

2. Give an example of how the Bible has helped you in your life.

3. How can the Bible be so simple yet so complicated at the same time?

4. Discuss using the Internet as a study tool. Talk about Bible dictionaries, encyclopedias, commentaries, atlases, and concordances. Do we need these study helps when we have access to a computer?

Map Search

• Find the land of Palestine on the map.
• Palestine was divided into three provinces. Name them, and find them on a map.
• On the east side of Palestine were three provinces. Name them and find them.
• Find the Mediterranean Sea.
• Find the Sea of Galilee and the Dead Sea.
• Find Bethlehem, where Jesus was born.
• Find the seat of government, which was Jerusalem.

Special Challenges

1. Learn to list in order and to spell the books of the New Testament.

2. Do some research about the period between the testaments and share with the class.

3. Make a commitment about Bible study.

4. Make a chart to share with the class of the categories of the books and/or writers.

5. Research, and write an introduction for each of the four gospels.

6. Do some research on Romans, Greeks, and Jews.

7. Make a poster/picture about the Word of God. You could use one of the verses in Psalm 150.

Suggestions for Teaching

Learning: Remember, students learn more when they become involved in the learning process.

Sharing: Have the class tell about a great Bible class they previously attended and how much they learned in the class. Always give students the option of saying, "I'm just glad to be here." Consequently, they won't feel uncomfortable or feel like they have to respond.

Prayer: Write prayer requests on the board or on paper before class and pray together.

Options

• Introductory activity to get to know one another: Divide the class into groups of four or five. Tell them that they are shipwrecked on the Isle of Cyprus. They only have materials that were taken from the ship to help them survive. Each must do his part to help the group survive. Make a list of what each person will contribute to the group. Include talents and experiences. Think in terms of spiritual, emotional, physical, and social welfare. Share with the class.

• Begin class by letting each member share a favorite New Testament book. Give them the option of saying, "I'm just glad to be here," if they don't want to share. This gives an easy way out and doesn't create anxiety. Usually it gets a laugh.

• If someone in the class has been to the Holy Land, you might let them share a short presentation.

• Review the fact sheet together and discuss the introduction. Encourage the class to do more research in these areas. Assign reports before the class convenes.

• Get into groups of two, and let the couples answer the questions and look up the places on the map.

- If time permits, you can do some of the challenges in class. You might work on the books of the New Testament together or make a chart of the books or categories. Announce that next week, the class will study the birth and early life of Jesus.
- The teacher and students might make character cards from 3 x 5 cards of characters that are studied each week. Put the name on one side in large letters and who they are on the back.
- The teacher could give a pre-test to learn how much students already know about the subject. Tell them not to put their name on the test but to put their test in a specific envelope upon completion so that no one will be intimidated.

The Bible and I

Oh, without the Bible,
How very poor I'd be.
Oh, without Jesus
No future I can see.
Life would have no reason
Just useless nights and days.
Living for myself—
No Lord who loves and saves.
Thank you God in heaven
For guiding men to write
About the life of Jesus
That gives us love and light.

Karen Robertson

The Bible

The Bible is the one that navigates me,
And teaches me how I ought to be.
It cheers, comforts and sustains,
Reprimands, corrects and explains.
My life is molded afresh every day,
Oh, how His Word can be such a way.
The Bible is not just any ole' book,
Read it every day and there is a brand new look.
How awesome is our God to write,
This Holy book that's never dull of light.

Glenda Beasley

Chapter Two

Birth and Early Life of Jesus

Fact Sheet

- We read of Jesus' birth and early life in Matthew and Luke only.
- Micah named Bethlehem as the birthplace of Jesus (Micah 5:2).
- Isaiah said that Jesus would be born of a virgin (Isaiah 7:14).
- Jesus was born in Bethlehem because Mary and Joseph went there to pay their taxes (Luke 2).
- Jesus was born in a stable because there was no room in the inn (Luke 2).
- Shepherds went to see Him (Luke 2).
- Wise men went to see Jesus after He had moved to a house (Matthew 2).
- When Jesus was presented at the temple, two turtledoves were offered for Him. Leviticus says that if a family was too poor to offer a lamb, they could offer two birds instead (Luke 8, Leviticus 12:8).
- Joseph takes Mary and Jesus to Egypt when Herod was going to kill all the boy babies two years old and younger (Matthew 2).
- When Jesus was twelve years old, Mary and Joseph took Him to Jerusalem (Luke 2).
- Jesus was missing, and His parents found Him in the temple talking with the religious leaders there (Luke 2).
- Jesus told His parents, "Did you not know that I must be about my Father's business?" (Luke 2:49).
- Temptations given by the devil: turn stones into bread, jump off the highest point of the temple, and bow down to Satan. Jesus withstood all temptation and rebuked Satan with Scripture. (Matthew 4).

- John the Baptist was born to Zacharias and Elizabeth before Jesus was born. He was a cousin to Jesus, and his job was to prepare the way for Christ (Luke 1).
- John baptized Jesus in the Jordan River (Matthew 3).

Outline of Jesus' Birth and Early Life

  I. Jesus is prophesied
 II. The Birth of John the Baptist, the Forerunner of Christ
III. Birth of Jesus in Bethlehem
 IV. The Shepherds Visit
  V. The Wise Men (Magi) Visit
 VI. The Presentation at the Temple
VII. The Flight to Egypt and Return to Nazareth
VIII. Jesus Goes to the Temple at the Age of Twelve
 IX. The Baptism of Jesus
  X. The Temptations of Jesus

Character List

Mary • Judah • Elizabeth • Simeon • Isaiah • Anna
Micah • The Herods • Joseph • John the Baptist • Zacharias

Map Search

Bethlehem • Judea • Egypt • Nazareth • Galilee
Jordan River • Jerusalem • Dead Sea • Sea of Galilee

Short-Answer Questions

1. The New Testament was written in what language?
2. Which gospel writers tell of Jesus' birth?
3. Which gospel is different from the others?
4. To whom were each of the gospels written and how was Christ presented in the book?
5. Name the eight writers of the New Testament and the categories of the books.
6. Name two foreign women in the genealogy of Christ (Matthew 1).

7. Which prophet foretold where Jesus would be born?

8. Which prophet said that Jesus would be born of a virgin?

9. Which Herod killed the boy babies in Bethlehem?

10. Who were the man and woman in the temple when Jesus was presented?

11. Name John's parents.

12. What was unusual about John's birth?

13. From which tribe were Mary and Joseph?

14. How do Matthew's and Luke's genealogy differ?

15. On what day was Jesus circumcised?

16. What gift did Jesus' parents bring to the temple?

17. In what river was Jesus baptized?

18. What was John's diet and what did he wear?

19. Name the three temptations the devil gave Jesus.

20. Name the three provinces of Palestine.

Thought Questions

1. How would you have felt in Mary's or Joseph's place? How would you tell your mother/father about the pregnancy?

2. "Mary found favor with God" (Luke 1:30). Could you substitute your name for Mary's? _____ found favor with God. Would God have chosen you to be the mother or father of the son of God?

3. Joseph was a poor man. Where do you think he got the money to take the family to Egypt?

4. Jesus had no sin. Why was He baptized?

5. "For with God nothing is impossible" (Luke 1:37). It was possible for Mary to have a baby when she had not had sexual relations with a man. How can you apply this principle to your life?

6. Mary pondered all these things that were happening in her heart (Luke 2:19). What things do you ponder in your heart?

7. What lessons can you learn from this study?

Application

Jesus was tempted in three ways. First John 2:16 says that all that is in the world is the "lust of the eyes, lust of the flesh, and the pride of life." How do these three principles apply to Jesus' temptations? Did these three principles apply to Adam's and Eve's temptation in the Garden of Eden? What about today? What temptations do we face that fit these three categories? How can we overcome temptations?

Elizabeth was pregnant at the same time as her cousin Mary. Elizabeth called Jesus "Lord" while He was still in the womb. Elizabeth proclaimed a blessing to Mary and called her the "Mother of my Lord" (Luke 1:43). There is no indication that there was any jealousy on Elizabeth's part. She knew Mary's son would be greater, but she did not mind. What about us today? Sometimes we compare babies and want our child to be the smartest, best-looking, and most athletic in a group. Could we learn a lesson from Elizabeth? Think about these things.

Assignment: Choose one of the special challenges.

Action Guide: The Bible says that nothing is impossible with God (Luke 1:37). What have you found impossible in your life? Could you still make things possible with God as your helper? Think about these things this week. Write or sing the words to your favorite song about Jesus' birth.

Special Challenges

1. Draw a picture of the three temptations of Jesus (Matthew 4).
2. Write a song about Mary or Elizabeth to the tune of "Mary Had A Little Lamb" or "Three Blind Mice."
3. Tell one of the stories listed in the outline to the class.
4. Write a skit about one of the stories listed in the outline. Direct class members in acting it out.
5. Find other Old Testament Scriptures about the prophecy of Jesus.
6. Research "Herod the Great" and "Herod Archelaus." Report to the class the information you find.
7. Make character cards as we progress through the twenty-

seven books. Write or type the names in large print on a card. On the back, write who they are. Work on the character cards each week.

8. Memorize Isaiah 9:6.

Suggestions for Teaching

Sharing: Let students tell about a time when a child or a relative was born. Share the excitement.

Prayer: Write prayer requests on the board, and pray for one another. Refrain from spending your study time discussing the sick. Maybe that could be done after class.

Options: Introduce the stories as listed. Look some of them up in the Bible and discuss, or put students in groups of two and let them discuss the outline.

- The birth and early life of Jesus.
- Discuss the application and thought questions.
- Emphasize the character list and map search.
- Encourage students to take some of the special challenges and/ or do some of them in class.
- Encourage students to read Matthew 1-4 and Luke 1-3.

ANGELS SANG AT HIS BIRTH

To Tune of "Lullaby and Goodnight"

Long ago, there was born
In the city of David
A sweet Holy Baby,
Who was Jesus, our King.

Chorus

Angels sang at His birth.

Lullaby, peace on earth.

Angels sang at His birth.

Lullaby, peace on earth.

-Author Unknown
(Encourage students to write other verses.)

Chapter Three

Teachings of Jesus

Fact Sheet

Jesus came to seek and save the lost. He began His ministry when He was 30 (Luke 3:23), and the ministry continued for about three years.

Jesus was the Master Teacher. Some of His characteristics as a teacher were:

- He loved his students.
- He was interested in His students.
- He knew the importance of His work.
- He knew the Scriptures.
- He knew his objectives.
- He used visuals and objects.
- He was a good storyteller.
- He prayed for His students.
- He prepared for His teaching.
- He used inquiry and discussion.
- He listened to His students.
- He taught application in His lessons.
- He evaluated.
- He took time for private devotion.
- His teaching was stimulating.
- He met individual needs.
- He trained teachers.
- He taught response.

Jesus used the following teaching methods: parables, questions (more than 1,000), lecture and discussion, problem solving, and conversation. He used objects (loaves, fishes, sky, money, fig tree, little child, etc.) in His teaching. He often taught one-on-one, and sometimes He taught groups. He sometimes used similes, which is a comparison using "like" or "as." Example: The kingdom of heaven is like.... Sometimes He used metaphors, which is a comparison without the use of "like" or "as." Example: I am the vine, you are the branches.

Jesus chose twelve men to help Him in His work. Later Paul was called an apostle, and Matthias was chosen to take Judas's place.

Character List

Peter • Andrew • James • John • Philip • Thomas
Matthew • Judas • Bartholomew • Simon • James, the less
Paul • Thaddaeus • Matthias (replaced Judas)

The Apostles

Peter: Son of Jonas, also called Cephas, name means "rock," from the cities of Bethsaida and Capernaum; a fisherman; brought to Christ by his brother, Andrew; part of Jesus' inner circle; denied the Lord three times, wrote two epistles (1,2 Peter), preached the first sermon on the Day of Pentecost; and was crucified in Rome upside down, according to tradition.

Andrew: Son of Jonas; brother of Peter; from the cities of Bethsaida and Capernaum; a fisherman; a disciple of John the Baptist; brought his brother Peter to Christ; brought the lad with five loaves and two fish to Jesus to feed 5,000 men; died as a martyr according to tradition.

James: son of Zebedee and Salome; brother to John; brothers called "sons of thunder"; fisherman from Bethsaida, Capernaum, and Jerusalem; part of Jesus' inner circle; first apostle martyred; beheaded by King Herod (Acts 12).

John: son of Zebedee and Salome; brother to James; brothers called "sons of thunder"; fisherman; from Bethsaida, Capernaum, and Jerusalem, part of Jesus' inner circle, called himself "the apostle Jesus loved"; Jesus asked him to take care of His mother; wrote five New Testament books (Gospel of John, 1,2,3 John, Revelation); banished to the isle of Patmos where tradition says he died a natural death.

Philip: Name means "lover of horses"; from Bethsaida; when Jesus called Philip, Philip called Nathanael and brought him to Jesus; according to tradition, died a martyr's death.

Bartholomew: Also called Nathanael; from Cana; made statement when learning about Jesus: "Can any good thing come out of Nazareth?"; Jesus saw him coming and said, "Behold, an Israelite in whom there is no guile"; Jesus saw him under the fig tree; according to tradition, died a martyr's death.

Thomas: Also called Didymus, from Galilee, once stated, "Let us go with Jesus and die with him." After the resurrection, he doubted, but later confessed Him by saying, "My Lord and my God."

Matthew: Also called Levi; son of Alphaeus; from Capernaum; a tax collector; wrote the book of Matthew to the Jews and presented Jesus as a king; according to tradition, died a martyr's death.

James: Sometimes called "the less"; son of Alphaeus; from Galilee; according to tradition, died a martyr's death.

Thaddaeus: Also called Jude, Judas, Lebbeus; from Galilee; according to tradition, died a martyr's death.

Simon: Known as the Zealot; from Galilee; according to tradition, died a martyr's death.

Judas: Called Iscariot; from Judea; treasurer of the group; traitor who betrayed Jesus with a kiss for thirty pieces of silver; called a "thief"; when he saw Jesus was condemned, he tried to return the money; hanged himself.

Matthias: Not one of the twelve; took Judas's place; chosen by the apostles as one who had companied with them from Jesus' baptism to His ascension and a witness of His resurrection; according to tradition, died a martyr's death.

Paul: Not one of the twelve; name changed from Saul to Paul; from Tarsus; tentmaker; educated under Gamaliel; persecuted believers then dedicated his life to teaching others about Jesus; made three missionary journeys and was a prisoner in Rome; according to tradition, was martyred.

Map Search

Jesus taught in Judea, Samaria, and Galilee. Find these three provinces and the Sea of Galilee, Jordan River, the Dead Sea, and the Mediterranean Sea.

Artist/designer Unknown

PETER
His name means stone.
He is standing on the stone.
He had keys to the kingdom.
Rooster-reminds him of three denials.

PETER

ANDREW

ANDREW
Fisherman-eating fish.
"Brought one" button- He brought
Peter to the Lord.
Book-tells others about Jesus.

JAMES
He has fishing pole-fisherman.
First martyr-looking at his
tombstone.

JOHN

JOHN
Has fishing pole-fisherman.
Valentine-apostle of love.
"Mother" tattoo—took care of
Jesus' mother.

JUDAS

JUDAS
Keeper of the moneybag.
Noose-hanged himself.

SIMON

Simon the Zealot
"Down with Rome" T-shirt
Zealots hated Rome. Wearing
guerilla warfare—was a
revolutionary

MATTHEW
Jeans-known as Levi.
Tax Form--tax collector.
IRS-Imperial Roman Servant.
He was a Jew working for
the Roman government.

THOMAS
Question marks--doubting Thomas.

JAMES THE LESS
Yardstick--trying to measure up

PHILLIP
Fill'er up--Phillip.
Phillips 66 gas station.

MATTHIAS
Straw--drew lots--he got short straw
Shoes--he had to fill Judas' shoes.

NATHANAEL
Also same as Bartholomew.
Fig tree--Jesus saw him there.
Bottle--no guile--what Jesus
said about him.

PAUL
Trunk – missionary journeys
Typewriter – more NT books
written by him than anyone
Lions Sport Bag – went to big
game in Rome

THADDAEUS
Three coats--had three names.
Could not decide who to be--
what to wear.

Short-Answer Questions: Who Am I?

Name the Apostle

1. _____ I was a tax collector.
2. _____ My name means "rock."
3. _____ I brought my brother to Christ.
4. _____ Two of the apostles had this name.
5. _____ Jesus first saw me under a fig tree.
6. _____ I had the "keys of the kingdom."
7. _____ We four were fishermen.

_____ _____ _____

8. _____ We were brothers. _____
9. _____ I was the "doubting one" because I didn't believe Jesus arose.
10. _____ We were sons of Zebedee.
11. _____ I denied Christ three times.
12. _____ I betrayed Christ with a kiss.
13. _____ I was the treasurer of the group.
14. _____ I was the revolutionary one.
15. _____ My other name was Simon.
16. _____ I hanged myself.
17. _____ Jesus told me to take care of His mother.
18. _____ I was the first apostle to die for the faith. Herod killed me.
19. _____ I took Judas's place.
20. _____ We three were Jesus' closest apostles.
21. _____ I wrote five books of the New Testament.
22. _____ I had at least three names.
23. _____ We were not part of the original twelve.
24. _____ I had no guile (evil) in me.
25. _____ We were called "sons of thunder."

Thought Questions

1. Why do you think Jesus chose the men He did to help Him? Wouldn't we have chosen the brightest and the most educated to help with a big project?

2. What characteristics of Jesus would we like for today's Bible class teachers to have?

3. Do you think Jesus would have used computers, projectors, and tablets if He were teaching us today?

4. Jesus often had to use "forbearance" when He was dealing with the apostles, like the time they wanted to be the greatest in His kingdom or even at His ascension (Acts 1) when they were still asking when He would restore His kingdom. Do we practice forbearance in our dealings with others?

Application: Jesus' mission was to teach, and then He gave the commission to the apostles and to us as well. Think about how you are teaching others about Christ. Are you teaching adults, teens, children, someone on the street, someone you know, etc.? Think about doing more to spread the Good News of Jesus.

Assignment: Learn to spell and write the names of the apostles.

Action Guide: The apostles went everywhere teaching.

Teach a child or grandchild or other relative something about Jesus this week. Write a thank-you note to a special teacher this week and thank him/her for teaching.

Special Challenges

1. Study the apostles and make a list of what you can learn about them.

2. If you don't already know it, learn the children's song about the apostles.

3. Make a chart about the apostles.

Suggestions for Teaching

Sharing: Name a favorite teacher and tell why he/she is your favorite or say, "I'm just glad to be here."

Prayer: Write prayer requests on the board or a handout and pray together.

Options

- Discuss Jesus' characteristics as a teacher and compare the list to the characteristics of teachers today.

- Discuss the twelve apostles and their characteristics.

- Divide into groups of two and give each group half a piece of poster paper, and assign them one of the apostles about whom to make a poster. For some like Peter, there will be lots of information on the poster, and for others like James, the Less, there will be little.

- Work on the short answer, matching, and thought questions.

- Play a game of "Who Am I?" with the apostles. Always play with groups instead of individuals.

- Divide the class into groups of two and have them discuss the apostles with the pictures in the book and answer the "Who Am I?" questions.

Review Questions (Chapters 1-3)

1. Name the three provinces in Palestine.

2. Where was Jesus baptized?

3. In what city was Jesus born?

4. In what city did Jesus grow to be a man?

5. How many years between the end of the Old Testament and the beginning of the New Testament?

6. What contributions did the Romans make to the cause of Christ?

7. Between the testaments, the Old Testament was translated from _____ to _____ .

8. Name the three eras of time, tell how long each lasted, and tell how God dealt with His people during each age.

9. Give three ways we can know that the Bible is the Word of God.

10. _____ wrote more New Testament books than any other.

11. Luke wrote _____ and _____ .

12. Name the five books that John wrote.

13. There are _____ books in the Old Testament and _____ in the New Testament.

14. The first four books of the New Testament are called

    _____ .

15. The book of Acts is a book of _____ .

16. The twenty-one books beginning with Romans are

    _____ or _____ .

17. Matthew presented Christ as a _____ , Mark presented Jesus as a _____ , Luke presented Jesus as a _____ , and John presented Jesus as a

    _____ .

18. Matthew wrote to _____ , Mark wrote to _____ , Luke wrote to _____ , and John wrote to _____ .

19. The gospel of _____ is different from the other gospels.

20. _____ and _____ tell of Jesus' birth.

21. Which of the gospel writers tell of Jesus' death?

22. Name the eight writers of the New Testament.

23. In what language was the New Testament written?

24. What sea is to the west of Palestine?

25. What prophet named the place where Jesus would be born?

26. What prophet said that Jesus would be born of a virgin?

27. There were three wise men. True or False.

28. Which Herod killed the boy babies in Bethlehem?

29. Name two foreign women in the lineage of Christ.

30. Name the two people in the temple who saw the baby Jesus.

31. _____ and _____ were John's parents.

32. Who first called Jesus "Lord"?

33. John was _____ older than Jesus.

34. From which tribe were Joseph and Mary?

35. Name the three temptations of Jesus.

36. When Mary and Joseph came back from Egypt, which Herod was ruling?

37. Name three teaching methods that Jesus used.

38. Name the 12 apostles, plus two extra.

39. Where were Joseph and Mary when the wise men saw Jesus?

40. Name four lessons we can learn from this material.

Apostles' Song

Jesus called them one by one,
Peter, Andrew, James, and John.
Next came Philip, Thomas too.
Matthew and Bartholomew.

Chorus

Yes, Jesus called them. (repeat twice)
The Bible tells me so.

James, the one they called "the less."
Simon, also Thaddaeus.
The twelfth apostle Judas made.
Jesus was by him betrayed.

Chapter Four

Parables and Miracles

Fact Sheet

A parable is an earthly story with a heavenly meaning or the comparison of a familiar fact to a spiritual truth. Jesus' parables dealt with things (16% to 25%); plants (7% to 11%); animals (4% to 7%); and to humans (34% to 50%). Jesus spoke in parables because storytelling was effective, His time had not come to speak plainly, and He wanted to conceal truth from dishonest Jews. Storytelling is still an effective method of teaching today because it allows us to paint pictures with stories.

Jesus told parables about farming, plants, fishing, and sheep because these were the objects with which the people in His day were familiar. Today, if He were telling parables, they would probably be about computers, malls, cars, etc. Try your hand at writing a modern-day parable.

A miracle is a supernatural or unexplained happening. There were miracles of healing and of nature. Jesus healed many people because He was compassionate, and He performed miracles of nature like turning water to wine, calming the sea, or feeding 5,000 men with two loaves and a few fish.

Miracles were performed to help people, but they were also performed so that people might believe (John 20:30, 31). Jesus raised three people from the dead: Lazarus, Jairus' daughter, and the son of a widow from Nain.

The Gospel of John records no parables.

Pick out three parables and three miracles from these lists and talk about them or choose others.

Parables

1. The Sower (Matthew 13:3-23)
2. The Ten Virgins (Matthew 25:1-13)
3. The Leaven (Luke 13:20-21)
4. The Prodigal Son (Luke 15:11-32)
5. The Rich Fool (Luke 12:16-21)

Miracles

1. Lazarus from the dead (John 11:38-44)
2. Jesus walks on water (Matthew 14:24-33)
3. Five thousand men are fed (Matthew 14:13-21)
4. Ten lepers are cleansed (Luke 17:11-19)
5. Centurion's servant (Matthew 8:5-13)

Thought Questions

1. Why did Jesus perform miracles? Were they ever performed for personal reasons?
2. Why did Jesus speak in parables?
3. Can faith healers perform miracles today?
4. Sometimes we loosely use the phrase "that was a miracle." We say, "It was a miracle that I didn't fall," or "It was a miracle that I found what I was looking for." Are these things really miracles? Give examples of miracles.
5. Do you think people would believe if they saw miracles today? Remember, many of the Bible characters didn't. What about those who saw Lazarus raised from the dead?
6. Why didn't Jesus heal everyone while He was on the earth?
7. Who could perform miracles?
8. Were miracles ever performed to harm someone or something?
9. What does 1 Corinthians 13:8-12 say about miracles?
10. When I pray for a sick person, am I praying for a miracle?

Application

Study the story of The Lost Sheep—Luke 15:1-7. Talk about the importance of one individual in the eyes of God. God is concerned if one of us is lost. We are special to Him. Matthew 10:30 says that even the hairs of our head are numbered. Also, in Matthew 6:25-34 the Lord tells us that He takes care of the birds, and He will take care of us. We are much more valuable than the birds. Jesus says that He wants everyone to be saved (2 Peter 3:9). Discuss why we have poor self-esteem and what we can do about it. Let everyone write a list of things that he does well to help him feel better. Remember, God loves one little lost sheep.

Assignment: Read the parables and/or miracles this week. (There is usually a list in the back of your Bible.)

Action Guide: Write a letter or e-mail this week to someone who has low self-esteem and let her know how important she is to God. You can use The Lost Sheep as an example.

Special Challenges

1. Tell the story of one of the parables. Remember these rules: Give the Scripture reference, plan a visual of some kind, make good eye contact, use voice inflection in your story, give the spiritual meaning of the parable, and have fun telling the story.

2. Write a modern-day parable and give the meaning of your parable. Write about computers, phones, malls, shopping, cars, etc.

3. Make a sheep for each student and let them put a magnet on the sheep and put it on the refrigerator to remind each one of his importance.

4. Copy a list of parables and miracles (perhaps from the back of your Bible). Look at the list, and study some of the ones that are unfamiliar to you.

5. Let classes get in groups of four or five and act out some of the parables. Some props would enhance the skits.

Suggestions for Teaching

Sharing: Begin class by letting everyone share about a time they prayed for someone and their prayer was answered with a *yes* or a *no*.

Prayer: Take prayer requests and pray together.

Options

- Discuss the fact sheet and pick out several parables and miracles to discuss in class.

- You can assign parables the week before class and have students present them on the day you introduce this subject.

- Discuss the application with the class.

- Select some of the challenges to do in class.

- Discuss the thought questions with the group.

A Modern-Day Parable by Joetta Kelly. I attended a volleyball game where some young people were playing. When I arrived, a parent had paid my way. I sat on the bottom bench screaming encouragement to them. They hit the ball over the net and supported each other when they missed. One of the young people saved me when several errant balls were aimed at me. Our lives are like this volleyball game. We work as a team with God, Jesus, and Holy Spirit fighting against Satan. Just as a parent paid my way, Jesus paid our way. We also encourage one another in the kingdom. Just as the student protected me from the balls, Jesus will protect us from Satan's fiery darts or volleys every day.

Eyes on Jesus

There's a story in the Bible
Where a miracle takes place.
A man walks on the water,
When He looks Jesus in the face.

The ship that the disciples were in
Was being tossed in the sea,
And when Jesus suddenly appeared,
They did not know it was He.

Jesus went walking toward them
Into the middle of the sea,
And He told them who He was,
But they could not view Him clearly.

Peter then called out and said,
"Lord, tell me to come if it's you."
So Jesus spoke the word, "Come."
And Peter walked on the water too.

And Peter was too afraid
For the wind was still swirling about.
And when He began to sink,
Jesus caught him and chided his doubt.

When everyone was in the ship,
Worship of Jesus was begun.
The disciples then were saying
That it was true He was God's son.

We must keep our eyes on Jesus,
Every moment of every day.
Then our doubt can turn to faith,
As we seek to follow His way.

Mary Louise Dabbs

Chapter Five

Death, Resurrection, and Ascension of Jesus

Outline of the Last Days in the Life of Jesus

Thursday

(All stories are located in the last chapters of Matthew, Mark, Luke, and John)

I. The Last Supper

    A. Jesus washed the apostles' feet (John 13:1-17)

    B. The Lord's Supper (Matthew 26: 17-27; Mark 14:12-25; Luke 22:7-22)

II. In the Garden of Gethsemane

    A. Jesus prays (Matthew 26:36-46; Mark 14:32-42; Luke 22:39-46; John 17:1-16)

    B. The betrayal by Judas (Matthew 26:47-50; Mark 14:43-50)

    C. The arrest by the mob (Matthew 26:50-56)

III. The trials before the priests

    A. Annas (John 18:12-14)

    B. Caiaphas (John 18:24)

Friday

I. Before the Sanhedrin at early dawn

    (Matthew 27:52-66)

II. Peter denies Christ three times

    (Matthew 26:69-75; John 18:15-37)

III. Judas hangs himself

    (Matthew 27:1-5)

IV. Trials before the Roman rulers

  A. Pilate (Matthew 27:11-26)

  B. Herod (Luke 23:5-12)

  C. Pilate again
1. Dream of Pilate's wife
2. The scourging
3. Pilate washes his hands
4. The release of Barabbas
5. The mocking of the soldiers

  D. The things that were wrong with the trials
1. It was held at night.
2. A person couldn't be declared guilty with one judge.
3. The court couldn't decide against a man on the same day as trial.
4. There must be three witnesses against a person.
5. It was against the law to have a private examination.

V. Crucifixion and Death

  A. On the way to Golgotha Simon helps carry the cross. (Luke 23:26)

  B. Seven sayings on the cross (Matthew-John)
1. Father, forgive them for they know not what they do.
2. Today, you will be with Me in paradise.
3. John, My mother. Mother, your son.
4. My God, My God, why have You forsaken Me?
5. I thirst.
6. Into your hands, I commit My spirit.
7. It is finished.

  C. The crucifixion and superscription

  D. The robbers (the mocking)

  E. Jesus provides for His mother

Friday Afternoon and Evening

I. The death (3:00 pm)

A. Rocks were broken asunder.

B. Darkness covered the earth.

C. The centurion exclaimed, "Truly this was the Son of God."

D. Bodies arose from the dead (Some think this was at the resurrection.)

E. People smote their chests.

F. Veil in the temple was torn asunder.

II. The proof of the death (John 19:34)

III. The burial in the tomb of Joseph of Arimathea (Mark 27:57-60; Luke 23:50-54)

IV. Nicodemus anoints Jesus' body (John 19:38-42)

V. The guard is placed at the tomb (Mark 27:62-66)

Sunday Morning (Triumph and Glory)

I. The Resurrection

A. The visit of the women to the tomb (Matthew 28:1-10, Luke 24:1-8).

B. The visit of Peter and John to the tomb.

II. The Appearances of Jesus

A. Jesus appears to Mary Magdalene and the other women

B. The report of the guard.

C. The appearance to Peter and James (1 Corinthians 15:5-7).

D. The appearance to Cleopas and another.

E. The appearance to the 10 apostles. Thomas was not there.

F. The appearance to the 11 apostles a week later.

G. Jesus appears to the fishermen in Galilee.

H. The appearance to 500 at once (1 Corinthians 15:6).

Forty Days Later

I. Final Commission

A. Appearance at a mountain in Galilee.

B. Appearance on Olivet in Jerusalem.

II. Final Ascension

A. Jesus' exaltation to God's right hand.

B. The apostles return to Jerusalem.

Character List

Annas • Herod Antipas • Caiaphas • Pilate • Malchus
Simon • Judas • Joseph of Arimathea • Mary Magdalene
Nicodemus • Cleopas

Short-Answer Questions

1. Name the garden where Jesus prayed.

2. Which 3 apostles did Jesus take with Him in the garden?

3. Jesus was betrayed with a _____ .

4. _____ took a sharp sword and cut off _____'s ear.

5. Jesus was first taken to _____.

6. Next He was taken to _____.

7. _____ denies that he knows Christ and the _____ crows.

8. Why did Jesus appear before Pilate?

9. The Jews said that Jesus was guilty of_____.

10. Why was Jesus sent to Herod?

11. Judas _____ himself.

12. _____, the prisoner, was released instead of Jesus.

13. _____ anointed the body of Jesus.

14. _____ carried Jesus' cross part of the way.

Thought Questions

1. Judas betrayed Jesus; Peter denied Him. What will you do with Jesus?

2. What would make Judas betray his master and friend? What causes us to do wicked things?

3. Did God forsake Jesus while He was on the cross? Why?

4. Why is this one of the greatest stories in the Bible?

Match the following items

_____ 1. Joseph of Arimathea

_____ 2. Mary Magdalene

_____ 3. Herod

_____ 4. Pilate

_____ 5. Nicodemus

_____ 6. Peter

_____ 7. Judas

_____ 8. Caiaphas

_____ 9. Thomas

_____10. John

A. Jesus appears to her first after the resurrection

B. Anointed the body of Jesus

C. Washed his hands of this trial

D. Buried Jesus

E. Denied Jesus

F. Ruler of Galilee

G. Betrayed Jesus

H. One who doubted

I. High priest

J. Apostle assigned to care for Jesus' mother

Application

Jesus gave His life that our sins might be forgiven. What does this mean to you? Are you willing to give your life to Jesus? What are some of the things you can do to show Jesus your appreciation?

Assignment: From memory, name the events that happened at the death of Jesus beginning with Thursday and continuing through Sunday.

Action Guide: Make a list of something you will do for Jesus this week that you have never done before.

Special Challenges

1. Learn the seven statements that Jesus made on the cross.

2. Paint or draw a picture of the cross.

3. Name the six hearings and trials of Jesus.

4. Do research on Pilate and Herod Antipas, and report to the class.

5. Read the stories of Jesus' death and resurrection in all four of the gospels. (Remember, these accounts will be at the end of the books.)

6. Draw a tombstone and write your name on it. Under your name list how you want to the remembered. "Here lies _____ who will be remembered for

   _____ .

7. Write a song or poem about the death of Jesus.

8. Look up songs in the song book about the death of Jesus and list them.

9. Do research on Mount Olivet (where Jesus ascended).

Suggestions for Teaching

Sharing: Begin class by sharing one event in the life of Jesus that really touches your heart. Always give students the option of saying, "I'm glad to be here." instead of sharing.

Prayer: Write prayer requests on the board, and pray together for one another.

Options

- Read and discuss some of the events in the death and resurrection of Jesus.

- Stress the hearings and trials of Jesus.

- Discuss the meaning of what Jesus did for us.

- Make a chart of the tombstone (# 6 under special challenges.)

- Get in groups of four and discuss the thought questions and application.
- Have students partner together to discuss the following:
  - Things that went wrong at Jesus' trials
  - The last supper
  - In the Garden of Gethsemane
  - Peter's denials
  - All day Friday
  - The death, burial, and resurrection

Jesus Died for You and Me

Jesus died for you and me.
He was nailed to His cross at Calvary,
That you and I might be set free.
Our freedom from sin is why He came.
Let us praise His Holy name.
God's Son took our blame and shame.
Let us teach others that they may see,
That Jesus died for you and me.
Never let scoffers say He died in vain.
Let us be thankful that Jesus came,
And every day praise His Holy name.
He gave His life unselfishly,
Yes, Jesus died for you and me.

Caserine Bell

Chapter Six

The Early Church Acts 1-7

Acts 1-7

Luke is the author of Acts and he wrote to Theophilus, a companion of Paul and Luke. Luke uses the term *we* in this book (Acts 16:10; 20:6). Since he was a physician, Luke uses medical terms in the book.

Key phrase to Acts: History of the church

Background: The title suggests the activities of the apostles, although all their activities are not recorded. The book centers around Peter, a minister to the Jews, and Paul, a minister to the Gentiles. The book focuses on four geographical centers: Jerusalem, Antioch, Ephesus, and Rome. The book has two divisions:

Chapters 1-12 mark the history of the church up to the death of Herod.

Chapters 13-28 is an account of the labors of the apostle Paul. The book answers the question: What must I do to be saved? It also gives the history of the first 30 years of the church.

There are several beginnings in the book
- Beginning of the work of the Holy Spirit
- Beginning of gospel preaching
- Beginning of the church
- Beginning of the Christian dispensation
- Beginning of salvation
- Beginning of world-wide evangelism

Outline of Acts 1-7

Chapter 1: Last words of Jesus, His ascension, a new apostle

Chapter 2: The church begins, activities in Jerusalem

Chapter 3: Peter and John go up to the temple, crippled man is cured

Chapter 4: Peter and John are put in prison

Chapter 5: Ananias and Sapphira lie and die; the apostles are persecuted

Chapter 6: Seven servants are chosen to take care of the widows

Chapter 7: Stephen's sermon and death

Character List

Review the apostles

Theophilus • Gamaliel • Joel • Luke • Peter • Matthias
Stephen • John • Barnabas • Ananias and Sapphira

Map Search

Jerusalem

Short-Answer Questions (Acts 1-7)

1. _____ The book was addressed to him

2. _____ Author of Acts.

3. _____ Two men who healed the lame man.

4. _____ The man who stood up in the council and spoke about releasing the prisoners.

5. _____ How many became Christians the first day?

6. _____ The man who was known as "an encourager."

7. _____ How old was the lame man who was healed?

8. _____ The city where the church started.

9. _____ How many were gathered in the upper room on the day of Pentecost?

10. _____ The mountain from which Jesus ascended.

11. _____ How many days was Jesus on earth after His resurrection?

12. Acts is a book of beginnings. Name four things that began in Acts.

13. What are the two divisions in the book of Acts?

14. Name the two primary characters in Acts and primarily to what group of people did each preach?

15. Basically, what were the two qualifications given for an apostle in Acts 1?

16. What questions did the apostles ask Jesus before He ascended to heaven?

17. When the people cried to Peter, "What must we do?" what was Peter's answer?

18. What two things were people to receive when they obeyed what Peter told them?

Thought Questions

1. What is the kingdom of God? Are the kingdom and the church the same thing?

2. Name four lessons you can learn from Acts 1-7, and give the story that taught you the lesson.

3. Stephen was stoned. What was Stephen's attitude toward those who killed him? What should our attitude be toward those who mistreat us?

Application

Ananias and Sapphira lied about how much money they got from their land. They both fell dead when they told a lie. What about our honesty? Are you honest in all your dealings? What about telling "little white lies"? Is exaggerating lying? Is telling only half-truths lying? Great fear came upon the church. Can you understand why?

Jesus chose to save us through the church. Why do you think He did this? Why wasn't it an individual thing between a person and God? How can the church help a person?

Assignment: Read Acts 1-7 this week.

Action Guide: Find a story you have studied that teaches the following principles:

> • God loves His children.
> • God will take care of His children.

- God has a job for everyone to do for Him.
- Nothing is impossible with God.
- It is great to show hospitality.
- Jesus loves sinners.
- Jesus had great power.
- When God heals someone, it is important to give something back to Him.
- When one is in trouble, He needs the Lord.
- Forgiveness is a true Christian characteristic.

Special Challenges

1. Look up information about the Day of Pentecost. What was the purpose of the feast? How long did it last? What were the Jews required to do at the feast? Give your report to the class.

2. Write a poem about one of the following: Ananias and Sapphira, the beginning of the church, Peter the Preacher, or the stoning of Stephen.

3. Make a list of all the Old Testament characters that Stephen mentioned in his sermon in Acts 7.

4. Learn the outline of chapters 1-7.

5. Look up information on the council before whom Peter and John appeared.

Suggestions for Teaching

Sharing: Let the class share about a time when they encouraged someone. It could be a note, a pat on the back, showing hospitality to someone, a gift, etc. Remember, Barnabas was an encourager. Discuss ways we can encourage others today. Remember to give students the option of saying, "I'm just glad to be here."

Prayer: Have students write prayer requests on the board and pray together.

Options

- Begin by discussing the introduction.

- Discuss the stories. (Many will be familiar with many of the stories in Acts, so the discussion can be a review.)

- Talk about the Day of Pentecost.

- Answer questions or write poems in class.

- Divide into groups and role play the following stories: choosing a new apostle, the beginning of the church, Peter and John going to the temple, Ananias and Sapphira, Stephen's speech and death. (Some love to role-play, but others may not be comfortable.)

- Encourage students to mark key passages in their Bibles.

- Put the character names in a sack, and allow students draw one out and tell something about the character. You could put two students together, so no one would be intimidated.

A Great Day

The Pentecost Day had come.
It was a very special day.
Jerusalem was completely filled,
With people from far away.

The Jews had come to worship.
They found, oh, so much more—
The kingdom God had promised
So many years before.
Apostle Peter used the keys
Jesus had promised to him.
Inspired by the Holy Spirit,
He boldly preached to them.

Saying:
Jesus came performing signs
You are witnesses to those,
But you killed Him anyway,

In three days He arose!
Witnessing His resurrection,
We apostles now tell the story.
God raised Him from the grave,
And raised Him to sit in glory.
Many hearers were pricked in their hearts.
For they had killed their king.
"What shall we do?" they cried,
"To right this wicked thing?"

"Repent and change your ways.
Wash all your sins away.
You'll then be in His kingdom.
Where you'll live and worship and pray."

Three thousand used those keys.
They were baptized that very day.
Now added to His church
They would live life God's way.

Karen Robertson

Stephen

Now Stephen was a preacher of Jesus Christ,
One of the seven who was chosen to serve.
And he was so full of power and faith,
But he received treatment he didn't deserve.

He was accused of speaking against God,
And speaking against the holy place.
But when the council looked at Stephen,
It was like looking at an angel's face.

Then Stephen preached to the high priest,
And all the men and brethren around

He told the story of the Patriarchs,
And how Israel had turned God down.

Stephen called them stiff-necked,
Killers of prophets who foretold,
The coming of our Just One,
And Stephen was so bold.

They were furious with Stephen,
But he looked up at God's right hand,
And there he saw the open heavens,
And with God, stood the Son of Man.

Then with Saul standing by watching,
They stoned him; they were such angry men.
But as Stephen knelt there dying,
He said, "Lord, don't charge them with this sin."

Mary Louise Dabbs

Ananias and Sapphira

Ananias and Sapphira were husband and wife,
And had acquired a lot of land during their life.

People were hungry and with nowhere to stay,
Landowners and wealthy gave all they had to share
in the way.

Ananias and Sapphira said, "We'll do that too,
Except we will lie and keep some for me and you."

God is not pleased when to Him we lie,
So Ananias and Sapphira did before the people suddenly die.

Glenda Beasley

A game to play in class: Pictionary™

The teacher divides the class into teams and gives one person (in secret) on the team the name of some event studied. For example: Jesus walks on water. All teams are given the same event. When the teacher gives the instructions to begin, one person in the group draws the event until someone in the group guesses it correctly. The first team guessing the event is given a point, and the game continues by the teacher giving another person in the group a different event, and thus the game continues. Students learn while having fun.

Chapter Seven

Converting the Lost (Acts 8-12)

Outline of Acts 8-12

Chapter 8: Gospel in Samaria, The Ethiopian eunuch obeys

Chapter 9: The conversion of Saul (Paul), Raising of Dorcas

Chapter 10: The conversion of the first Gentile, Cornelius

Chapter 11: Peter tells about Cornelius' conversion

Chapter 12: King Herod kills James and puts Peter in prison

Character List

Ethiopian eunuch • Simon • Candace • Rhoda
Saul (Paul) • Ananias • Mary, mother of John Mark
Dorcas/Tabitha • King Herod Agrippa • Cornelius

Map Search

Jerusalem • Samaria • Ethiopia • Joppa

Short-Answer Questions

1. The apostles are spending their time preaching, and the _____ are being neglected.

2. The apostles chose _____ men to help them.

3. Two of the men chosen who we read about later were _____ and _____ .

4. The crowd became _____ when they heard Stephen preach.

5. They _____ him.

6. How do we first read of Saul (Paul)?

7. What did Stephen say to God about those stoning him?

Chapters 8-12

8. _____ was persecuting Christians and putting them in
   _____ .

9. Philip went down to _____ to preach there.

10. There he met a magician named _____ who wanted to
    _____ the gift of the Holy Spirit.

11. The magician was told to _____ and _____ .

12. God told Philip to go preach to the _____ , who was
    riding in a chariot.

13. The man had been to _____ , but he did not know Jesus.

14. The man wanted to be _____ after Philip preached to him.

15. Saul was on the road to _____ to kill Christians
    and put them in prison.

16. He saw a _____ and a voice who told him
    _____ .

17. _____ came and preached to Saul.

18. What did the minister tell him to do? (Acts 22:16)

19. Where did Paul go after he became a Christian for two
    years? (Galatians 1:17)

20. Peter raised _____ or _____ from the dead.

21. She lived in _____ .

22. She made _____ for other people.

23. The first Gentile person to become a Christian was
    _____ , who lived in _____ .

24. Describe the vision that Peter had.

25. Who did Cornelius have at his house when Peter arrived?

26. The people were called Christians first in _____ .

27. King Agrippa kills _____ and puts _____ in prison.

28. An angel lets _____ out of prison, and he goes to _____
    house where Christians are gathered.

29. How does King Herod Agrippa die?

30. _____ answers the door when _____ arrived.

Thought Questions

1. The Ethiopian didn't know much about Jesus when he became a Christian. How much does a person need to know today before he becomes a Christian?

2. Have you ever taught someone in a chariot, a car, or an airplane?

3. The Ethiopian went on his way rejoicing after he was baptized. Why was he so happy?

4. Dorcas did good deeds for others by sewing for them. What legacy are you building for yourself?

5. Paul changed his life drastically. How can a person change from taking drugs to teaching about the evils of drugs? From being a drunk to teaching others about drunkenness? From cussing to saying kind, sweet words? How can these dramatic changes take place?

6. Would you have been prejudiced against Cornelius if you had been there?

7. What lesson can we learn from Peter's vision?

8. Have you ever been to a prayer meeting like Mary was having at her house? What is the advantage of such a meeting?

9. Why did God send His Holy Spirit to Cornelius in a special way? Have we overcome prejudice today in the church?

10. Why does the Bible say that "Philip *went down* from Jerusalem to Samaria?" (Remember, Jerusalem was located on a hill.)

11. If you are saved, you want others saved. What are you doing now to save the lost? What will you do in the future to save the lost?

Application

Jesus died for every person and nationality. Each one is special in God's sight. The story of Cornelius teaches us this lesson. God has cleaned every person (Peter's vision), and we must not call anyone unworthy of the gospel. Think about what you can do to teach someone outside of your country or your class? Can you teach someone who doesn't live in your neighborhood or city? Can you go to the homeless, the less fortunate, or the poor? Jesus reached out to all people. Can we do less?

Assignment: Read Acts 8-12 this week.

Action Guide: These apostles suffered persecution, and were often put in prison. Write to a prisoner this week and try to encourage him. There may be someone in your church family with whom you could write, a relative, or ask someone for a name.

Matching

_____ 1. Philip   A. What Simon did before he became a Christian

_____ 2. chariot   B. Province where Philip preached

_____ 3. rejoicing   C. At whose feet those who stoned Stephen laid their clothes

_____ 4. Simon   D. What the eunuch wanted when he saw water

_____ 5. sorcerer   E. In what was the eunuch riding

_____ 6. Samaria   F. Book the eunuch was reading

_____ 7. Candace   G. Preacher in Samaria

_____ 8. Baptism   H. Tried to buy the gift of the Holy Spirit

_____ 9. Isaiah   I. How the eunuch went on his way

_____10. Saul   J. Queen of the Ethiopians

Review Matching: Acts 1-12

_____ 1. Chapter 1   A. Peter and John heal a man

_____ 2. Chapter 2   B. Cornelius becomes a Christian

_____ 3. Chapter 3   C. Stephen

_____ 4. Chapter 4   D. Herod puts Peter in prison

_____ 5. Chapter 5   E. Seven deacons

_____ 6. Chapter 6   F. Paul becomes a Christian

_____ 7. Chapter 7   G. Disciples are called Christians in Antioch

Special Challenges

1. Research the term *eunuch* and find out who they were and why they were eunuchs.

2. Conduct a study of *repentance.* Why is repentance so important?

3. Learn the outline of chapters 8-12. You will need to know this as you teach others.

4. Write a song about Paul becoming a Christian to the tune of "Mary Had a Little Lamb."

5. Do a study of the various Herods who lived during New Testament times.

6. There is so much misunderstanding about *baptism.* Use a concordance to find all the Scriptures about *baptism* and *baptize.* Answer these questions:

What is baptism? Who was baptized? Where were they baptized? When were they baptized? How were they baptized? What was the purpose of baptism?

Suggestions for Teaching

Sharing: Have the class share about the time they were baptized. So they won't feel uncomfortable, always give them the option of saying, "I am glad to be here."

Prayer: Write prayer requests and pray together.

Options

- Discuss the main stories in chapters 8-12.

- Encourage students to mark important passages in their Bibles.

- Discuss short answer and thought questions.

- Work on some of the special challenges in class.

- Put the following names/events in envelopes and let teams see who can put them in sequence the fastest: beginning of the church, Jesus goes back to heaven, Ananias and Sapphira, Peter is put in prison, Stephen is stoned, Paul becomes a Christian, the Ethiopian is converted, etc.

- Have students tear a piece of paper into some object that represents something in one of the stories in this lesson. Share with the class. For example: prison wall, bright light, etc.

Game to play in class: Word Association Game

Give teams a word, and tell them they must name events in the Bible that could be associated with the word. For example: *brothers* (they could name brothers in the Bible); *storm* (Paul in a storm, Jesus in a storm, Jonah, etc.); *sword* (Goliath's, David's, Samson's). This game is good for a review. It could be played on paper or orally.

Chapter Eight

Three Missionary Journeys (Acts 13-21)

Outline of Acts 13-21

Chapter 13   Paul, Barnabas, and John Mark begin the first journey from Antioch (two years)
They preach on Cyprus
John Mark turns back at Perga
Paul preaches in Antioch
Paul begins to preach to the Gentiles

Chapter 14   They preach in Iconium and are forced to leave
Healed a man at Lystra and were stoned
Appointed elders as they return home
Completed the first journey and reported to the church at Antioch

Chapter 15   Jerusalem Conference about circumcision

Chapter 16   Timothy, Silas, and Luke join Paul on the second journey (three years)
Lydia and her household are converted
Paul casts an evil spirit out of a girl
Paul and Silas are put in prison
The jailor is converted at Philippi
Paul and Silas are released

Chapter 17   Church grows under persecution
Church established in Thessalonica and Berea
Paul goes to Athens and preaches

Chapter 18   Paul makes tents with Aquila and Priscilla
Church is established in Corinth
Apollos corrected by Aquila and Priscilla
Paul completes the second journey

Chapter 19   The Third Journey (four years)
Paul preaches in Ephesus and the School of Tyrannus
for two years
Books of magic are burned
Demetrius stirred up riots

Chapter 20   Troas: Broke bread, Eutychus fell out the window
Miletus: elders from Ephesus met Paul

Chapter 21   Caesarea: Goes to the house of Phillip
Paul reports on his trip
Jerusalem: Paul is taken captive
Paul asks permission to speak

Character List

Paul • Philip's daughters • Aquila • Silas • Eutychus
Priscilla • Timothy • Demetrius • Apollos • Agabus
John Mark • Lydia • Barnabas • Jailor at Philippi • Luke

Map Search (Important places on the journeys)

Jerusalem • Antioch of Syria • Cyprus • Perga • Antioch of Pisidia
• Lystra • Philippi • Corinth • Athens • Troas • Thessalonica
• Berea • Ephesus • Caesarea • Miletus

Short-Answer

1. Three people who started on the first journey were
   _____, _____, and _____.
2. Who was the first convert in Philippi?
3. Why were the Bereans called noble?
4. What did Paul preach in Athens?
5. Name the couple with whom Paul lived.

6. What man knew only the baptism of John?

7. What happened to Eutychus?

8. Who was Agabus?

9. In what school did Paul preach in Ephesus?

10. What vision did Paul see in Troas?

Name the Place

1. _____ Timothy's home city

2. _____ City of Aquila and Priscilla

3. _____ Where Demetrius stirred up trouble

4. _____ Place from where Paul began his journeys

5. _____ Place where Paul met the Ephesians elders

6. _____ The city of the unknown god

7. _____ City where Eutychus fell out the window

8. _____ Where Philip and his daughters lived

9. _____ City where they stoned Paul

10. _____ Where Paul and Silas were put in prison

11. _____ City where Paul was taken prisoner

Thought Questions

1. Name some trials that Paul faced on his journeys. Are you willing to face trials to take the gospel to others?

2. Why is it important to have leaders/elders in the church?

3. Why is it sometimes good to part ways when you are having trouble getting along with someone or can't solve your relationship problems? Paul had this trouble with John Mark turning back on the first trip.

4. Why do you think Lydia wanted Paul and Silas to go home with her? Do you readily show hospitality?

5. Why did Paul tell the jailor to believe and that was the only instruction he gave him?

6. How can each of us be a missionary?

7. The people in Ephesus burned their magic books (worth a million dollars today) to become Christians. What do you need to give up in your life to follow Jesus? Money? Family? Career? Friends? TV? Sports? Movies? Music? Time? Food? What did Jesus mean when He said that we must deny ourselves and take up our cross and follow Him?

Application: These early Christians went everywhere teaching the good news of Jesus. Some obeyed; others didn't. That sounds like today. What are we doing to take the good news to the world? Are you giving money, grading correspondence courses, going to foreign places, working in the inner cities, or teaching your neighbor about Jesus? There is a song called "Must I Go and Empty-Handed." The song asks the question about how many souls we will take with us to meet Jesus or will we go empty-handed? Think about this.

Assignment: Read these chapters (13-21) and look at the teaching methods of Paul and his companions.

Action Guide: Teach someone about Jesus this week. You can teach a neighbor, a relative, a child, a class, or a friend.

Special Challenges

1. Look at a map and trace all three journeys. Learn what happened at the cities where Paul was visiting.

2. Read the words to the songs "Must I Go, and Empty-Handed" and "You Never Mentioned Him to Me."

3. Make a chart of what these people did to become Christians: On the Day of Pentecost (ch. 2), the Ethiopian (ch. 8), Paul (chs. 9, 22, 26), Cornelius (ch. 10), Lydia (ch. 16), and the jailor (ch. 16).

4. Write an essay on Paul the Apostle and His Great Work.

5. List characteristics of Paul that made him a great leader.

Suggestions for Teaching

Sharing: Have members of the class share a time when they taught someone about Jesus. It could be teaching a relative, a child, a neighbor, etc. Always allow them to opt out if they're uncomfortable participating by saying, "I'm just glad to be here."

Pray Together

Other Optional Activities

- Discuss Paul's journeys after giving a map to each student.
- Discuss the outline given in this lesson.
- Answer the short-answer and thought questions.
- Do some of the Special Challenges in this chapter in class.
- Encourage students to read the stories at home.

Chapter Nine

Paul's Journey to Rome (Acts 22-28)

Outline of Acts 22-28

Chapter 22   Paul Makes His Defense to the Jews

When about to be whipped, Paul identifies his Roman citizenship.

The Sanhedrin is called to meet.

Chapter 23   Paul Appears Before the Sanhedrin

Paul turns the Pharisees against the Sadducees in the Council.

The Lord tells Paul that he will go to Rome.

Plot of Jews to kill Paul.

Paul is sent to Caesarea.

Chapter 24   Paul Has a Trial Before Felix

Tertullus accused Paul of profaning the temple.

Paul makes his own defense.

Paul appears before Felix and Drusilla.

Felix trembled, saying he would call for Paul again.

Chapter 25   Paul Appears Before Festus

Paul is in bonds after two years.

Festus becomes governor.

Paul makes his defense before Festus.

Paul appeals to Caesar.

Festus wants Agrippa to hear Paul.

Chapter 26   Paul Appears Before Agrippa

Agrippa is almost persuaded to become a Christian.

Agrippa said that Paul may have been freed if he hadn't appealed to Caesar.

Chapter 27   Preparation of Journey to Rome

Julius was put in charge of Paul.

Paul was given some freedom.

A storm lasted for fourteen days.

Paul tells the crew they would be saved if they stayed in the ship (all 276).

They kept the prisoners alive because of Paul.

Chapter 28   The Shipwrecked on the Island of Malta

They built a fire and a viper bit Paul.

First, they thought he was a murderer and then they thought he was a god.

Publius, chief official, kept them 3 days.

Paul healed Publius' father and many others.

They stayed on the island for three months.

In Rome, Paul is allowed to live by himself with a servant.

From morning to evening Paul preaches.

He is there for two years.

He depends on Christians for his needs.

The book of Acts closes.

Paul's Last Days

The rest of the story is from history. There is a list of visitors and companions in Romans 16:3-24. Paul wrote Ephesians, Philippians, Colossians, and Philemon while in prison. We don't know why his record wasn't in Rome. Most think he was imprisoned later and killed by Nero. Paul said, "I have fought the good fight. I have finished the race. I have kept the faith (2 Timothy 4:7). "Rejoice and again I say rejoice" (Philippians 4:4).

Character List

Felix • King Agrippa • Julius • Drusilla • Bernice
Publius • Festus • Tertullus • Caesar

Map Search

Jerusalem • Malta • Caesarea • Rome

Short-Answer Questions

1. How did Paul escape the beating after he was captured?
2. How many men had a vow to kill Paul?
3. Name the lawyer who testified against Paul.
4. How many soldiers took Paul to Caesarea?
5. Of what did they accuse Paul?
6. Name the two rulers before whom Paul appeared whose names begin with "F."
7. _____ was the name of Paul's guard.
8. What was the name of the storm that came up at sea?
9. What was the message of the angel that appeared before Paul?
10. _____ (number) were on board Paul's ship?
11. Who was Publius and what did Paul do for him?
12. How long did Paul stay in the rented house in Rome?

Thought Questions

1. Paul appealed to Caesar. What does that mean?
2. Describe a person who is "almost persuaded" to become a Christian.
3. Why did Felix tremble?
4. Paul was such a strong Christian. Was there a chance he might fall away? (1 Cor. 9:27)
5. Can you see the providence of God in the life of Paul? He wanted to go to Rome and preach. He got a free trip. Has God worked something out with His providence in your life?
6. How did Paul feel about being a prisoner?
7. How did Paul get to be a Roman citizen? He didn't live in Rome.

Application

Bad things kept happening to Paul: He was taken prisoner; some men had a vow to kill him; he was thought to be a murderer and then a god; he was shipwrecked; and he was in prison for two or more years.

Yet, Paul had confidence and joy and looked at his life as a way to serve and teach others. Can you relate to this? Do you have joy in spite of troubles? Do you continue to serve and reach out to others with confidence in spite of trials?

Assignment: Read Acts 22-28, and think about Paul's life.

Action Guide: Write a paragraph about how you have overcome trials in your life. Share it with a group to encourage them.

Special Challenges

1. Find information on the Roman rulers: Felix, Drusilla, Festus, King Agrippa, and Bernice. You might also find some information on the Roman ruler, Nero.
2. Trace Paul's journey to Rome on a map.
3. Make a list of Paul's trials. See 2 Corinthians 11:23-33.
4. Write five lessons you can learn from Paul and share those lessons with the class.
5. Make character cards to study.
6. Make a timeline using the outlines at the beginning of the chapter to show what happened to Paul after he became a prisoner.

Suggestions for Teaching

Sharing: Share a time in your life when the circumstances looked bad, but they turned out for good.

Prayer: Take requests and pray together.

Options

- Discuss the outline of chapters 22-28.
- Trace Paul's journey to Rome on a map.
- Identify the people and places in the lesson.
- Share research with the class on the Roman rulers.
- Answer short answer and thought questions.
- Students can tear a piece of paper into some object to represent something in the story.
- Have someone write a skit about the shipwreck and act it out with the class.

Chapter Ten

The Epistles

21 Christian Letters

Written by: Peter, Paul, James, Jude, John

Written to: churches, individuals, and groups of churches

Individuals written to: Timothy, Titus, Philemon

Written to a Group of churches: Galatians

Revelation: Written by John (Book of hope)

Romans-Ephesians

1. Romans

Key phrase: The just shall live by faith (1:17).

Background: This book is written by Paul to the church in Rome. Paul had never been to Rome, but he wanted to go. Some think this book is Paul's greatest work.

Purposes: Paul had an interest in the church and had a great desire to visit them in the near future. He wanted to prepare them for his visit. Paul wanted the Romans to have a thorough grounding in the doctrine of faith and grace. Phoebe was going to Rome, so Paul had an opportunity to send the letter.

Interesting Points

- This is a book of questions and answers.
- This is a book of doctrine.
- Paul provides a list of sins (1:29-32).
- Paul writes good rules about living the Christian life (ch 12).
- Application (8:28, 31, 35, 37-39).
- Woman in Romans: Phoebe, who will deliver the letter for Paul (16:1-2).

- List of people Paul knew in Rome (16:3-16).

Several Things He Wrote About
- Why Christ had to die
- Why the Church was established
- Why the wrath of God is upon man
- Why sin must be punished
- Why Jesus was rejected
- Summary of Christian living

Formula for Salvation
- Romans 3:23 All have sinned.
- Romans 5:12 Sin brings death.
- Romans 5:7,8 Christ died for sinners.
- Romans 6:3-4 We can be baptized into Jesus and walk in newness of life.

Thought Questions
1. Salvation is a gift, as recorded in Romans 4. We don't work our way to heaven. Since this is true, why do people work for the Lord?

2. Paul begged these Romans to pray for him (15:30-31). Have you asked someone to pray for you? Do you ask often?

3. Paul says that all the commandments could be summed up in "love your neighbor as yourself." He reminds us that adultery, murder, stealing, and coveting are all covered in love. How is this possible? (Romans 13:9-10)

4. Paul gives us a list of practical suggestions for living. On which suggestion do you need to work? (Romans 12)

5. Memorize Romans 8:28, and keep it close to your heart. It is a special promise.

6. Gaius had been showing hospitality to Paul and the whole church, (Romans16:23). What do you think that Gaius was doing to show hospitality? Do we show enough hospitality today?

Map Study: Find Rome and Corinth (place from which Paul was writing).

1 Corinthians

Written from Ephesus by Paul to the church in Corinth to help them with their problems.

1. **Key Phrase:** Problems in the church
2. **Background:** Paul was in Corinth on his second journey for over a year and a half, staying with Aquila and Priscilla. While he was in Ephesus, Chloe reported to Paul the trouble that the church at Corinth was having
3. (1 Corinthians 1:10-17). Paul wrote to help them with the problems.

Some of the Problems of the Church

- Divisions (1:10-17)
- Marriage (chapter 7)
- Lawsuits (6:1-8)
- Food offered to idols (chapter 8)
- Immorality (5:1-13)
- Questionable practices
- Abuse of the Lord's Supper (11:17-26)
- Spiritual gifts (chapters 12-14)

Suggested Scriptures to Note

3:5-11	6:18-20
3:16-17	10:1-13 (Old Testament example)
5:9-11	

Outline of 1 Corinthians

   I. Introduction and Benefits of Being in Christ (1)

  II. Division (1-4)

 III. Immorality in the Church (5-6)

 IV. Marriage (7)

  V. Liberty and Worship (8-14)

A. Food Sacrificed to Idols (8)

B. The Rights of an Apostle (9)

C. The Lord's Supper (10-11)

D. Head Coverings (11)

E. Gifts (12)

F. Love (13)

G. Prophecy and Tongues (14)

VI. Resurrection (15)

VII. Collection and Conclusion (16)

2 Corinthians

Written from Macedonia by Paul to the church in Corinth to defend his apostleship.

Key phrase: Paul as an apostle

Background: Jewish party gained strength and challenged the authority of Paul. Paul wrote this letter to defend his apostleship, conduct, and character. He had sent Titus to set things in order.

Outline of II Corinthians

I. Salutation and Greeting (1:1-2)

II. Paul Affirms His Sincerity (1-7)

III. The Appeal for Separation from Heathenism (6-7)

IV. Collection for the Poor Saints at Jerusalem (8-9)

V. Paul Defends His Apostleship (10-12)

VI. Final Exhortation and Greeting (13)

Paul's Qualifications

1:8-11   10:12-18   2:12-17   11:5-12

4:7-18   11:22-33   6: 3-12   12:7-13

Special Challenges for 1, 2 Corinthians

1. Make a list of Paul's qualifications for being an apostle.

2. Read 2 Corinthians 9:6-9 and discuss sowing, reaping, and giving.

3. Make a list and discuss Paul's hardships (2 Corinthians 6:4-6).

Galatians

Written from Corinth by Paul to the region of Galatia.

Key phrase: Free from the law

Background: This book was written to the country of Galatia. This is the only one of Paul's books that is written to a group of churches. Paul was in Galatia on all three of his missionary journeys. Peter may also have been there (1 Peter 1:1). The date of this writing is really unknown. Some believe this was the first book Paul wrote, and others think it was the last.

Purpose: Jewish teachers had come into the country and insisted upon formalism and legalism. They insisted that Christians must keep the old law of separation of Jews from other people. Paul wrote this letter to let them know that they were unshackled from the law.

Suggested Scriptures to Note

1:8-9
2:11-16
3:1-6, 11
5:19-26 Works of the flesh, Fruits of the Spirit
6:1-2, 7, 9

Outline of Galatians

I. Paul, the Apostle (1-2)
II. Doctrinal Principles (3-4)
III. Freedoms and Privileges (5-6)
IV. Conclusion (6)

Thought Questions

1. In writing to the Galatians Paul said that there were prejudiced people back in this day, and the Jews wanted the gospel for themselves. Paul shows numerous times in his letters that the gospel was for all. Are you prejudiced against anyone: whites, blacks, Jews, Iranians, Chinese, etc.? There is no place in God's

kingdom for prejudice. God loves everyone and wants everyone to be saved. Search your heart.

2. Underline and look at Galatians 3:28, which is an important verse. What do you think it means?

Ephesians

Written by Paul from prison in Rome to the church in Ephesus.

Key Phrase: Building Up the Church

Background: Ephesus was the chief city of Asia, one of the seven churches of Asia. They worshiped the goddess Diana (Artemis). All the roads from east to west went through Ephesus (Acts 19:10). Paul stayed in Ephesus for more than two years on the third missionary journey and taught in the School of Tyrannus. Many of the people burned their books of magic and became Christians. Demetrius, the silversmith, stirred up the whole town and started a riot about their goddess. On his return to Jerusalem, Paul met with the elders of Ephesus at Miletus and encouraged them. They cried as he left because he told them they would see his face no more.

Purpose: Paul had no particular reason for writing. Tychicus was taking the letter to Colosse; therefore, he could take this one by Ephesus. Paul had a deep love for the Ephesians. It involves no controversy and deals with no particular problem. Some think that this letter was circulated among the churches and written in a general way so it would be helpful for all the churches.

Outline of Ephesians

 I. The Salutation (1)

 II. Exhortations Concerning the Grace of God (1-3)

 III. Exhortations to Christians (4-6)

  A. Unity

  B. Morality

  C. Christian family

  D. Christian warfare

 V. The Conclusion (6)

Suggested Scriptures to Note

1:7, 16, 22-23	5:3-5 list of sins
2:8	5:16-21
3:20	6:1-4
4:1-6	6:13-18 Armor of God
4:25-32	

Thought Questions

1. Paul said that he had doubts about these people. What does that mean? Do you have doubts about your church? Why?

2. All spiritual blessings are in Christ. What about people who aren't in Christ? How do they get these blessings?

3. What is our sinful nature?

4. If we are saved by grace, why must we repent and be baptized?

5. Gentiles were once far away, but we can be one in Christ. Can Mexicans, Jews, Gentiles, Chinese, Russians and Italians be one in Christ Jesus? How is this possible?

6. Paul encourages the Ephesians to not be discouraged. What discourages us today? When you get discouraged, what do you do?

7. God prepares wonderful things to happen that we cannot even imagine. Have you ever had something wonderful happen that you could not even imagine happening in your life and it took you by surprise?

Characters from Romans-Ephesians

Paul • Chloe • Tychicus • Aquila • Phoebe • Demetrius Priscilla • Titus

Suggested Activities

I. Class Activity Divide the class in groups of two and give them a slip with one of the "Suggested Scriptures to Note" on it. You can also give them posterboard, paper, and markers to use to present their lessons to the class.

Example: Take the following Scripture/s and teach us what God is telling us. You can give background, meaning, examples, and admonitions for today. You may write, list, or draw on your paper to help us get the meaning of the verse/s.

II. Class Activity: Read about the works of the flesh and the works of the Spirit in Galatians 5:19-26. Write these words on strips of paper and tape or pin them on one of you. One can take the works of the flesh and the other the works of the Spirit. Explain what the words mean. You can assign one group or many groups. Feel free to make this exercise dramatic.

III. Class Activity: Copy a picture of a man in armor for each member of the class. Have each student label the picture with the armor given in Ephesians 6:10-20. Explain what the armor is about and talk about the war that Christians are fighting

Application: Choose lessons from "Suggested Scripture to Note."

Assignment and Action Guide: Read these five books, take notes, and share lessons with the class.

Teaching the Epistles

Sharing: Share about a time when you lived in another place and wrote to some of the people there after you left. Some may have lived in one place all their lives. They can share a time when someone wrote to them.

Pray together

Options

Look for the following with each book:
- Author
- Keyword/phrase
- Purpose of writing
- Background information
- Scriptures to note (you may wish to select your own Scriptures)
- Answer the questions
- Complete the activities
- Do a map study
- Discuss application lessons

Chapter Eleven

Philippians-Titus

Philippians

Written by Paul from prison in Rome to the church in Philippi.

Key Word: Rejoice or joy

Background: The Philippian church was the first in Europe. Paul visited Philippi after receiving the Macedonian call (vision) in Troas. Lydia and her household were the first converts there, and the jailer and his family gave their lives to the Lord. Epaphroditus traveled from Philippi to Rome to take Paul supplies.

Purpose: Paul was writing to the people to thank them for the offering they had sent him for his missionary work. Paul had accepted money from them twice.

(Philippians 4:16-18). He was thankful for these brethren and used the word *joy* or *rejoice* 16 times in the book. There is no condemnation in this book except for the admonition to the two women in Philippians 4:1-2 to "be of the same mind."

Outline of Philippians

    I. Salutation (1)
   II. Situation and Labors of Paul (1-2)
  III. Warnings Against False Teachers (3)
  IV. Exhortation (4)

Suggested Scriptures to Note

2:9-11, 14-18, 3:12-16, 4 (whole chapter)

Colossians

Written by Paul from prison to the church in Colossae.

Key phrase: Christ is above all.

Background: Colossae was a city in Phrygia. The people were in the audience on the Day of Pentecost (Acts 2:10). We do not know if Paul had ever been to Colossae from Colossians 2:1. It was the home of Epaphras and Philemon. Ephesians portrayed the church of Christ, and Colossians portrays the Christ of the church. Paul also wanted this letter read in Laodicea (Colossians 4:16).

Purpose: False teachers had brought their philosophy into the church which said Christ was good as far as He went, but He wasn't complete. They worshiped angels. Epaphras, the minister, was disturbed and wanted Paul's help. Paul wrote to show that Christ was preeminent in everything and the Christian life should reflect that priority and to instruct the church concerning false teachers.

Divisions:
Chapters 1-2 doctrinal

Chapters 3-4 practical

Suggested Scriptures to Note
Colossians 1:23

Colossians 2:11-14

Colossians 3:5-17 (put off, put on)

Suggested Class Activities

Class Activity
In Colossians 3, there are things that we should put on and things we should put off. Make some strips of paper of these words and demonstrate to the class by taping these words on someone or on a board. You can make this dramatic, which will help others to remember the words.

Short-Answer on Romans-Colossians
1. The epistles were written to _____ and

    _____.

2. Individuals written to were _____, _____, and_____.

3. Give the key phrase for each book:

Romans_____

1 Corinthians _____

2 Corinthians _____

Galatians _____

Ephesians _____

Philippians _____

Colossians _____

4. _____ wrote Romans and probably 1 and 2 Corinthians on the _____ missionary journey.

5. Give the background of the following books:
   - Romans
   - 1 Corinthians
   - 2 Corinthians
   - Galatians
   - Ephesians
   - Philippians
   - Colossians

6. How did Paul get the letter to the Romans?

7. Give the purpose of each book.

8. Name at least three problems the church in Corinth was having.

9. List the armor of God as listed in Ephesians 6.

10. List the things that we are to put off and put on as given in Colossians 3:5-17.

11. List the things on which we are to meditate from Philippians 4:8-9.

12. Write the works of the spirit and the works of the flesh as listed in Galatians 5:19-25.

13. List four hardships that had happened to Paul since he became a Christian.

1, 2 Thessalonians

Written from Corinth by Paul to the church in Thessalonica. Maybe two of the earliest books written.

Key phrases: 1 Thessalonians: stay on target

2 Thessalonians: second coming of Christ

Background: Paul, Silas, and Timothy established the church at Thessalonica on the second journey (Acts 17). After Paul left Philippi (prison), they went to Thessalonica. For three Sabbaths, Paul reasoned in the synagogue. The Jews stirred up the people and attacked the house of Jason. Paul and Silas were sent by night to Berea.

Purpose: Persecution was taking place, and Paul thought the Christians would fall back into their old ways. Paul had learned that the Christians were being disturbed by rumors of the early return of Christ. He admonishes some of them for stopping their work and living in idleness and advises all of them to be ready by working quietly and hard with patience and faith. They thought Jesus was coming soon, and they sold their goods and quit working.

Outline of 1 Thessalonians

    I. Salutation

    II. Paul's Personal Thoughts (1-3)

    III. Paul's Exhortation (4-5)

    IV. Conclusion (5)

Outline of 2 Thessalonians

    I. Salutation (1)

    II. Commendation and Doctrine (1-2)

    III. Exhortation (3)

    IV. Conclusion (3)

Interesting Scriptures to Note

1 Thessalonians 4:1-11, 16-17

1 Thessalonians 5:14-28

2 Thessalonians 1:7-12; 3:6-14

1, 2 Timothy

Written by Paul to his son in the gospel, Timothy

Key phrases: 1 Timothy: Leadership

2 Timothy: Overcoming evil

Place of writing: It is thought that Paul was released from his first imprisonment and was able to travel. Maybe Paul wrote 1 Timothy during this time. Most believe that 2 Timothy was written during his second imprisonment. Maybe 2 Timothy was the last book written. These deductions are usually taken by using the links in these two books.

Background: Paul probably met Timothy's family on his first missionary journey. Timothy's mother, Eunice, was a Jew, and Timothy's father was a Greek. On the second journey when he came by Lystra, Timothy's home, Paul invited Timothy to go with him (Acts 16:1-5). Paul first circumcised Timothy because his father was a Greek. The Bible says that Timothy's mother and grandmother (Eunice and Lois) taught Timothy the Scriptures from the time he was a child (2 Timothy 1:5; 3:15). Timothy also accompanied Paul on the third journey. Paul had urged Timothy to stay in Ephesus and help the church there. Paul calls Timothy his beloved son in the Lord.

Purpose: Paul is writing to instruct Timothy in things that were necessary for him to set things in order in Ephesus. He was facing false doctrine, and leadership needed to be developed. He instructed him to be on guard and not to let his youth become a liability.

Second Timothy is a letter of encouragement. Paul warns Timothy that his teaching will come under attack but he has Paul's example to guide him and God's Word to fortify him. Paul tries to comfort and sustain Timothy. Paul wants Timothy to come to Rome and bring John Mark with him. Paul also wanted Timothy to bring the cloak, the books, and especially the parchments. He wanted Timothy to come before winter (2 Timothy 4:11, 21).

Outline of 1 Timothy

Chapter 1: Greeting and Reminder of Charge

Chapter 2: Public Worship

Chapter 3: Qualifications of Deacons and Elders

Chapter 4: Special Advice to the Ministry

Chapter 5: Duties of Elders, Older Women and Widows

Chapter 6: Relationships of Slaves to their Masters

Outline of 2 Timothy

   I. Salutation and Greeting (1)

  II. Paul's Concern for Timothy (1-2)

 III. A Pattern for a Man of God (2)

     A. Paul

     B. Soldier

     C. Athlete

     D. Farmer

     E. Jesus

     F. Worker

     G. Vessel

     H. Servant

 IV. Exhortations and Instruction (3-4)

  V. Conclusion (4)

Scriptures to Note:

- List of sins: 1 Timothy 1:8-11, 18-21
- Role of Women: 2 Timothy 2:8-15
- Qualifications of Bishops, Elders, Overseers, and Deacons: 1 Timothy 3:1-13
- Latter Times: 1 Timothy 4:1-8
- 1 Timothy 5:8, 17-18; 6:6-17
- 2 Timothy 1:5; 2:15, 22-24; 3:1-2, 16-17; 4:2,7-8

Titus

Written by Paul after his first imprisonment to the young man named Titus.

Key Phrase: Instruction and Encouragement.

Background: This book is written to a young man named Titus, who Paul called his true son in the faith. Titus is a Gentile, which probably meant that his parents were Gentiles. Titus takes Paul's second epistle to Corinth. Paul instructs him to complete the collection (2 Corinthians 8:5-7). Titus and Paul are together on Crete. It is thought that Paul has been released from prison the first time, and now his second trial is pending (Titus 1:5). Paul leaves Titus on Crete to set things in order and appoint elders (Titus 1:5). Titus receives the letter from Paul. Paul tells Titus to wait for Artemas and Tychicus, and when they arrive to come to him at Nicopolis where he is spending the winter. Titus becomes a watchword of the Cretans. His greatest work will be there. Most think that Titus joined Paul in Rome and was there during his last days, but we cannot be certain of this. Paul says of Titus: "Titus is my partner and fellow worker concerning you" (2 Corinthians 8:23).

Purpose for Writing: Paul writes to instruct Titus about the work in Crete and to encourage him. He instructs Titus about the high standards for church leaders and the need for sound doctrine and practical Christian living.

Outline of Titus

Chapter 1: Precepts for congregational life

      A. Elders are to be appointed in each town

      B. They should be well-qualified—gives qualifications

Chapter 2: Precepts for family and individual life

      A. Older men—older women

      B. Younger men—younger women

      C. Christian teacher—Christian workman

      D. The grace of God

Chapter 3: Precepts for social life

      A. The Christian citizen

      B. Showing kindness

      C. Rejecting quarrelsome and factious people

      D. Final Greeting

Interesting Scriptures to Note

1:5-9 (Qualifications of elders)

2:2-12 (Instructions for men and women)

3:9-11 (Avoid dissension)

Application: There are many verses that can be taught for application. Pick a set of verses from these books that would be helpful to your church. Philippians 2:3-9 is a good place to start.

Assignment: Read Philippians-Titus through this week.

Action Guide: This week be kind, tenderhearted and forgiving to all you meet and share with the class next week (Ephesians 4:32).

Special Challenges for the Epistles

1. Paul wrote letters to encourage the early Christians. This week write five notes to someone you know who needs encouraging.

2. Learn to identify the list of characters listed in the back of the book.

3. Plan a devotion on one of the epistles and present it to the class.

4. Make a chart of the epistles. Include key phrase, purpose, background, etc.

5. Read the epistles. Take notes or write down things that you want to remember.

6. Set a goal about doing more Bible study.

7. Interview four Christian ladies. Design questions that would help you live the Christian life.

8. Develop a self-improvement project that would help you to grow as a Christian. Share with the class to encourage them.

9. Paul encouraged the brethren to pray for one another. Keep a prayer journal and include a list of people for whom you would like to pray.

10. Develop a set of evangelism charts that one could use to teach someone the gospel.

11. Research Titus.

Characters from Philippians-Titus

Epaphras • Lois • Philemon • Eunice • Timothy • Titus

Class Activity

Divide the class in groups of two and give them a slip with one of the "Suggested Scriptures to Note" on it. You can also give them posterboard, paper, and markers to use to present their lessons to the class.

Example

Take the following Scripture/s and teach us what God is telling us. You can give background, meaning, examples, and admonitions for today. You may write, list or draw on your paper to help us get the meaning of the verse/s.

Teaching the Epistles

Sharing: Paul was a friend of many of the people with whom he wrote. What makes a good friend? Let each one share a characteristic that a good friend possesses.

Pray together

Options

Look for the following with each book:

- Author
- Keyword/phrase
- Purpose of writing
- Background information
- Scriptures to note (you may wish to select your own Scriptures)
- Answer the questions
- Complete the activities
- Do a map study
- Discuss application lessons

Games that can be played in class

Name the Character: Divide the class into two teams or more and let each team name a Bible character. The next team must then name one that begins with the last letter of the previous character. If a team can't name one, then the other team gets a point, and you can begin again. Also, if a team repeats one that has already been named, the other team scores.

Twenty Questions: The teacher thinks about something that is being studied. The teacher identifies it as animal, vegetable, or mineral. The team gets 20 questions to guess what the teacher is thinking. They can ask questions that can be answered with *yes* or *no*.

Tic-tac-truth: The teachers/students write questions in nine categories and make or draw a tic-tac-toe board. Categories could be characters, New Testament, Old Testament, quotations, who is speaking, judges, kings, miscellaneous, spelling, geography, or numbers. Play like tic-tac-toe. The class could also play Jeopardy with the categories, using questions worth 10, 20, 30, or 40 points.

Chapter Twelve

Philemon-Revelation

Philemon

Written by Paul from prison to Philemon who lived in Colosse.

Key Phrase: The slave Onesimus.

Background: Slavery was common in the Roman Empire, and some early Christians had slaves. The letter does not deal with the problem of slavery, but gives the Christian approach of dealing with a present social evil. Philemon, a wealthy slave owner, had been converted by Paul. Onesimus, one of his slaves, ran away and was converted by Paul in Rome. The letter was not entirely private as it would probably require the help of Apphia, Philemon's wife, and Archippus, his son, and the church in Philemon's house. Paul felt that Onesimus must return to his master and make restitution. Tychicus was dispatched with the letter, and Onesimus also carried the letter to the Ephesians and Colossians.

Outline of Philemon

- Salutation 1-3
- Thanksgiving for Philemon 4-7
- Entreaty for Onesimus 8-21
- Paul's personal affairs 22-24
- Benediction 25

Hebrews

The author is unknown, but the book is generally attributed to Paul. The writer does not give the author's name either in the greeting or in closing salutations. The writer was well-known by those whom he addressed. The benediction reads like other writings from Paul.

Written to: Hebrew Christians, probably Hebrews in the Gentile lands, instead of the Christians in Jerusalem. In the letter, the author states that these Christians were being persecuted and were in danger of being tempted to fall away.

Key Phrase: Growing in the faith

Background: The Hebrews had questions about Christianity, and the writer tries to answer them. They were looking for evidence that their new faith was genuine. The Jews had the miracle of crossing the Red Sea and the Jordan River on dry land. They had the law given at Mt. Sinai, beautiful worship services, a temple, and a priest to offer sacrifices so they could be forgiven. What did the Christians have? How could this new faith forgive sins and encourage friendship with God? The writer wants to let the people know how important Jesus really is.

Purpose: To show them the excellence of Christ and that Christianity is superior to Judaism. The writer shows that Christ is superior to prophets, angels, Moses, and Joshua. Christ's priesthood is superior to Aaron's. Then he shows them that the new covenant is superior to the old covenant. He exhorts them in steadfastness built on their faith and examples of faith.

Outline of Hebrews

I. A Better Messenger: Christ (1-2)

II. The Better Apostle ((3- 4)

III. The Better Priest (4-7)

IV. The Better Covenant (8 -9)

V. The Better Sacrifice (10-12)

VI. The Better Way: Faith (10-12)

VII. The Practice of Faith (13)

James

Author: There are three men with the name of James in the New Testament. James, the son of Zebedee, James, son of Alphaeus, and James the half-brother of Jesus.

It is usually thought that this author is James, the half-brother of Jesus.

Key Phrase: Living with a working faith.

Written to: The twelve tribes (Jewish Christians) scattered abroad. Persecution had come, and the Christians scattered.

When Was It Written: Some think this was the first New Testament book written, while others disagree. There is no mention of the controversy over Gentiles, and this leads some to think that the letter was written before Gentiles became Christians.

Background: It is thought that Jesus' brothers did not believe in Him during His personal ministry because of John 7:5. Jesus appeared to James after his resurrection and all doubts were removed (1 Corinthians 15:7; Acts 1:14). James played an important role in the early church. He is mentioned several times in Acts, and Paul referred to him as one of the "pillars" of the church at Jerusalem (Galatians 2:9). In this letter, he identifies himself as a servant of the Lord Jesus Christ (1:1).

Purpose: James knew of the severe trials these saints had to endure for their faith. He wrote to encourage them and warn them against being lax in their duties. The main ideas are Christian wisdom, good works, and pure religion. It lays out the premise that: "Faith without works is dead."

James is one of the most practical books of the New Testament, and is one that is needed by all Christians. He shows Christians how faith is to be lived in the total arena of life. The book gives practical wisdom.

Outline of James

    I. True Religion in a Time of Trial (1:1-18)
    II. How Our Faith Is Tested in This World (1:19-5:18)
    III. Restoring the Erring (5:19-20)

Scriptures to Note

1:5-6, 25-27   3:1-12   2:17-26   4:7-8   13-17
Many others, practical 5:16-20

1 Peter

Written by the Apostle Peter to Christians all over Asia Minor (Pontus, Galatia, Cappadocia, Asia, and Bithynia).

Key Phrase: Persecution.

Written from: Babylon probably before the destruction of Jerusalem.

Purpose: Peter was writing to Christians who were being persecuted. He was letting them know that suffering can be a way of serving the Lord, of sharing the faith, and of being tested. They would suffer more, but it should make them glad because it will strengthen their faith and bring them honor when Christ returns. He reminded them that when they suffered, they were sharing in Christ's sufferings. He also wrote to encourage them to be strong.

Outline of I Peter

I. Greetings and Prayer 1:1-2

II. A Real Reason for Hope 1:3-12

III. Living as God's Holy People 1:13-2:17

IV. The Example of Christ's Suffering 2:18-25

V. Being a Christian and Suffering 3:1-4:19

VI. Advice for Church Leaders 5:1-11

VII. Final Greetings 5:12-14

Key Scriptures to Note

1 Peter 2:9
3:1-4, 8-15, 20-21
4:11, 16
5:1-4, 7

2 Peter

Written by the apostle Peter. The book was a general epistle and was not written to any person or group.

Key phrase: The coming of false prophets

Purpose for writing: The purpose was to warn of the coming of apostasy. He warns them that false prophets and teachers had entered the Christian community and were trying to lead the Lord's followers from the truth.

Outline of 2 Peter

I. Greetings and Prayer 1:1-2

II. How the Lord's Followers Should Live 1:3-15

III. The Glory of Christ 1:16-21

IV. False Prophets and Teachers 2:1-22

V. The Second Coming of the Lord 3:1-13

VI. Exhortations 3:14-18

Scriptures to Note

2 Peter 1:4-7, 21

2 Peter 2:1, 20-22

2 Peter 3:9-15

1 John

A general epistle written by the apostle John, from Ephesus.

Key Phrase: Faith and Love.

Background: Some people had come in to the church and were teaching Gnosticism, which is a combination of Paganism and Christianity. They denied Jesus came in the flesh. *Gnosticism* means "to know" and the word *know* is used 40 times in this book. John wrote them to encourage and to keep them from sin.

Purpose: Paul wrote to help Christians with their faith and love. John wrote to meet the doctrinal and practical needs of his hearers. He wanted believers to know that when we tell God about our sins, God will forgive us and take them away. The true test of faith is love for each other. Because God is love, His people must be like Him. For a complete victory over sin, we must not only love others, but we must believe that Jesus, the Son of God, is truly Christ, and that His death for us was real.

Suggested Scriptures to Note

1:7-10   2:15-17 3:18-19 4:1, 7-21   5:14

2 John

Written by John, the apostle. With only one chapter, it is the shortest book in the Bible.

Written to: The elect lady and her children. Some think this was a lady, and some think it was the church.

Key phrase: False teachers in the church.

Purpose: False teachers were going from place to place preying on the churches. This letter warns against showing hospitality to such false teachers. He writes about the importance of love in a Christian's life.

Outline of 2 John

    I. Signature and Salutation (1-4)

        A. John's love for the faithful

        B. Appreciation for their loyalty

    II. Admonitions (5-6)

        A. To walk in love

        B. To keep the commandments

    III. Warnings (7-11)

        A. Deceivers were abroad

        B. The deceivers identified

        C. Those who go beyond what Jesus taught have not God

        D. Such are not to be received into one's house

        E. To shelter false teachers is to partake of their evil works

    IV. Conclusion (12-13)

        A. Expectation of an early visit

        B. Salutation from an elect sister's children

Interesting Scriptures: 1:4-6, 9

3 John

This single-chapter book was written by John, the apostle, to Gaius. We do not know who Gaius was. Four times there is a Gaius mentioned in the Bible: Acts 19:29; 20:4, Romans 16:23, and 1 Corinthians 1:14. We do know that he was loved by Paul, and Paul was thankful for the things he did.

Key Phrase: False teachers and workers.

Purpose: Warns against false teachers, but says that we must support those who go to other parts of the world to tell others about Jesus.

Outline of III John

    I. Salutation (1-4)

A. Author's prayer for Gaius' health

B. Satisfaction on hearing that Gaius walked in truth

II. Encouraging workers for truth (5-8)

A. They go forth for the sake of the Name

B. They take no support from unbelievers

C. The church's duty to support them

D. Those who go forth share in the blessings of the work

E. Mutual cooperation implied

III. Reproving Opponents of Truth (9-10)

A. Diotrephes used ugly words against the apostle and believers

B. Forced the church to reject the letter the apostle wrote

C. Excluded from fellowship those who did receive Paul

D. Gaius is one of those exalted

IV. Faithfulness of Demetrius (11-12)

V. Letter Written to Encourage Gaius (13)

VI. Closing Salutations (14)

Interesting Scripture: 1:4

Jude

A single-chapter book written by Jude, the half-brother of Jesus, to Christians.

Key Phrase: Contending for the faith.

Purpose: Jude writes to tell Christians to defend the faith against false teachers. He says that false teachers are evil, God will punish them, and Christians shouldn't imitate them in the way they live.

Outline of Jude

I. Introduction (1-4)

A. Salutation (1, 2)

B. Occasion for writing (3, 4)

II. Appeals to historic precedents for examples of condemnation (5-7)

III. Arraignment of apostate teachers (8-16)

A. Wicked and good contrasted (8-10)
B. Condemnation of evil-doers (11-13)
C. Prophecy of Enoch (14-16)
IV. Exhortation to faithfulness (17-23)
V. Benediction (24-25)

Interesting Scripture: Jude 3, 21, 24-2

Revelation

Written by John, the apostle who was exiled on the Isle of Patmos.

Key Phrase: John's visions.

Background: Revelation is the only book of prophecy in the New Testament. On the isle of Patmos where he was exiled, John saw visions about God's message and Jesus Christ.

Purpose: The purpose of the book is to show Christian "victory." He wanted to encourage Christians to resist the cult of emperor worship and to stand firm during persecution. Jesus, born in a manger, is now triumphant over Satan. And we, the soldiers, are assured of victory, and Christians know the end of the story. The best is yet to be. Our leader is the King of kings, the Lord of lords and the Mightiest Prince of all. Let us march!

The message has three main parts:

- There are evil forces at work in the world.
- Christians may have to suffer and die.
- Jesus is Lord, and He will conquer all people and powers.

Revelation is a book of visions. The author uses many powerful images to describe God's power and judgment.

Application of Philemon through Revelation

James discusses the tongue and how we use our tongues in the wrong way. Think about the things you have said this week. Did you lie, swear, curse, or take God's name in vain? Did you built and encourage others with your tongue?

First John is a book that discusses loving God and others. Think about how you show love to others and how you can love the people who are hard to love.

Assignment: These books talk about how we need to grow in faith. Make a list of things we can do to grow our faith.

Action Guide: Work on answering the review questions in chapter 13.

Short-Answer Questions

Give keyword/phrase, writer, background and purpose of each of the following books:

Philemon _____

Hebrews _____

James _____

1, 2 Peter _____

1, 2, 3 John _____

Jude _____

Revelation _____

Thought Questions: Philemon-Revelation

1. Why did Paul want Onesimus to go home to Philemon after he became a Christian?

2. Hebrews discusses the old covenant and the new covenant and says that we live under the new covenant. Why do many people still want to live under the old covenant?

3. James is a practical book. Give one practical lesson that you can learn from James.

4. Do you think that Americans will ever suffer persecution as Christians? Are you ready to stand the test?

5. Second Peter, 2 John, and Jude talk about our being aware of false prophets. How can you tell a false prophet from a true one?

6. First John has much to say about loving God and loving others. Some people are easy to love, and others, like the selfish, cowards, greedy, and envious, are hard to love. How do we love the unlovely?

7. Name five books in the Bible with only one chapter. Remember, one is in the Old Testament.

8. How can we do a better job of living the principles found in the epistles?

9. Make a list of five lessons that were meaningful to you in this study.

Characters

Philemon • Apphia • Archippus • James, Jesus' brother
Gaius • Jude, Jesus' brother

Special Challenges

1. Make a chart of these books naming author, keyword/phrase, background, and purpose.

2. Make a list of questions you could use to ask about Christian living from these books.

Class Activity

Divide the class in groups of two and give them a slip with one of the "Suggested Scriptures to Note" on it. You can also give them posterboard, paper, and markers to use to present their lessons to the class.

Example

Take the following Scripture/s and teach us what God is telling us. You can give background, meaning, examples, and admonitions for today. You may write, list or draw on your paper to help us get the meaning of the verse/s.

Teaching

Sharing: Let each student tell about something that he/she is looking forward to in heaven.

Prayer: Pray for one another

Options

Look for the following with each book:

• Author
• Keyword/phrase

- Purpose of writing
- Background information
- Scriptures to note (you may wish to select your own Scriptures)
- Answer the questions
- Complete the activities
- Discuss the application
- Do the assignments and actions guide

Game that could be played in class: The teacher puts the letters of the alphabet in an envelope and then draws one out. Each team must name one person, place, or thing from the Bible that begins with that letter. Go around as many times as possible until neither team can name something. The other team scores if they can't name something. For example, the letter *A*. Students could name Adam, Athens, Aaron, Antioch, etc.

Chapter Thirteen

Review

I. Key Phrases to Remember

Matthew: Jesus is king

Mark: Jesus is a servant

Luke: Jesus was a perfect man

John: Jesus is God

Acts: History of the church

Romans: The just shall live by faith

1 Corinthians: Problems in the church

2 Corinthians: Paul, an apostle

Galatians: Free from law

Ephesians: Building up the church

Philippians: Rejoice

Colossians: Christ is above all

1 Thessalonians: Stay on target

2 Thessalonians: Second coming of Christ

1 Timothy: Leadership

2 Timothy: Overcoming evil

Titus: Instruction and encouragement

Philemon: The slave, Onesimus

Hebrews: Growing in the faith

James: Living with a working faith

1 Peter: Persecution

2 Peter: Coming of false teachers

1 John: Faith and love

2 John: False teachers in the church

3 John: False teachers and workers

Jude: Contending for the faith

Revelation: John's vision

II. Review the introduction

1. How many books are in the New Testament?

2. Name the writers.

3. Name the three eras of time in Bible history.

4. What events happened between the testaments that helped Christianity spread?

5. The Gospels: Give the author, to whom written, and how Jesus was presented in the book.

6. In what language was the New Testament written?

III. Identify the Following Characters

Matthew

Mark

Luke

John

Peter

Paul

James

Jude

Micah

Isaiah

Mary

Joseph

Zacharias

Elizabeth

Andrew

Philip

Bartholomew

Ananias (taught Paul)

Matthias

Paul

Lazarus

Annas

Caiaphas

Herod the Great

Herod Archelaus

Herod Antipas

Aquila

Priscilla

Stephen

Philip

Titus

Thomas

James, son of Alpheus

Thaddaeus

Mary (John Mark)

Lois

Eunice

Tychicus

Epaphras

Timothy

Joel

Ethiopian

Cornelius

Candace

Onesimus

Jude

Demetrius

Eutychus

Philip's daughters

Agabus

Simon of Samaria

Chloe

Phoebe

Archippus

Apphia

Gaius

James (brother to Jesus)

Artemis

Diana

IV. Find the following places on a map and identify the significance of the place.

Palestine	Joppa
Jordan River	Ethiopia
Dead Sea	Iconium
Mediterranean Sea	Cyprus
Sea of Galilee	Perga
Jerusalem	Patmos
Antioch	Lystra
Bethlehem	Miletus
Thessalonica	Galatia
Judea	Colosse
Samaria	Malta
Galilee	Philippi
Nazareth	Troas
Egypt	Crete
Ephesus	Colosse
Rome	Tarsus
Corinth	Damascus
Berea	Caesarea
Athens	

V. Identify the writer, key phrase, purpose, and background of each New Testament book.

VI. Review the questions in the previous chapters.

VII. Write as many lessons as you can that come from the New Testament. Be sure to list the story that teaches the lesson.

My Class

Twenty-seven Books in Thirteen Weeks

My class makes learning fun,
We even have tidbits before class has begun.
I never feel uncomfortable, you see
Because learning the Bible is good for me.

When we go through the New Testament story,
Sometimes I begin to fret,
But I have learned not to get upset,
Because everyone sometimes forgets.

Our class has a unique way of making you feel at ease.
We laugh at each other's mistakes,
When our answers are not just right,
We thank God for His light.

I am so grateful for this class,
Sometimes we sing our way through the Word.
The great Bible truths on which our class looks
Brings me much closer to the Book.

The New Testament study has been made easy,
So there is no reason for me to feel queasy.
I just follow the lead and continue to read,
So that I can go forth and plant the Seed.

Each week I know I will be blessed,
By the knowledge this class does possess.

I have been blessed beyond measure.
I feel blessed to share this treasure.

We have gone through maps and charts.
That showed us where the apostle Paul went.
He survived many awful perils,
But was protected by the Holy Spirit whom God sent.

To this class, I will never be able to properly thank you,
For all that you have meant to me.
I can only say, "Thank you, Thank you."
And to God I thank too.

Caserine Bell

Twenty-seven Books in Thirteen Weeks

120 Points
Final Exam/Open Book Quiz

Name _____ Date _____

I. Identify the following characters: (1 point each)

1. _____ prophet who said Jesus would be born of a virgin.

2. _____ prophet who said Jesus would be born in Bethlehem.

3. _____ tribe of Joseph and Mary.

4. _____ ruler who killed the babies of Bethlehem.

5. _____ ladies and man in the temple who saw baby Jesus.

6. _____ John the Baptist's parents.

7. _____ apostle who was a tax collector.

8. _____ apostle who was given the keys to the kingdom.

9. _____ apostle who was the first to die for the faith.

10. _____ apostle who brought his brother to Christ.

11. _____ four fishermen who were apostles.

12. _____ apostle who doubted the resurrection.

13. _____ apostle who took Judas' place.

14. _____ apostles who were called _____ "sons of thunder."

15. _____ apostle who was told to take care of Jesus' mother.

16. _____ apostle who wrote five of the New Testament books.

17. _____ man who wrote more books than any other man.

18. _____ two high priests who heard Jesus.

19. _____ woman of whom Jesus cast out seven demons.

20. _____ man whose ear was cut off in the garden.

21. _____ the Herod who tried Jesus

22. _____ the Herod who tried Paul.

23. _____ man who anointed the body of Jesus.

24. _____ man who carried the cross part of the way for Jesus.

25. _____ Roman ruler who turned Jesus over to be crucified.

26. _____ the writer of Acts.

27. _____ to whom the book of Acts was written.

28. _____ two who started on the first journey with Paul.

29. _____ one who started on the second journey with Paul.

30. _____ man known as the "encourager."

31. _____ prophet whom Peter quoted on the Day of Pentecost.

32. _____ apostle to the Jews.

33. _____ apostle to the Gentiles.

34. _____ two who lied about the money _____ given to the apostles.

35. _____ man baptized on the way to Gaza.

36. _____ woman who had a prayer meeting at her house.

37. _____ the Herod who killed James.

38. _____ first Gentile Christian.

39. _____ woman Peter raised from the dead.

40. _____ first Christian martyr.

41. _____ man who taught the eunuch.

42. _____ man who turned back from the first journey.

43. _____ woman who became a Christian in Philippi.

44. _____ man and his household who became Christians in Philippi.

45. _____ man who taught Paul the gospel.

46. _____ sorcerer who tried to buy the gift of the Holy Spirit.

47. _____ man who stirred up a riot in Ephesus.

48. _____ couple from Corinth.

49. _____ two young men who traveled with Paul (his gospel sons).

50. _____ prophet who said Paul would be taken in Jerusalem.

51. _____ man who had four daughters who prophesied.

52. _____ man who fell out the window when Paul was preaching.

53. _____ man who kept Paul as a prisoner.

54. _____ woman who delivered the letter to the Romans.

55. _____ two women who were fussing in Philippi.

56. _____ slave whom Paul wrote a book about.

57. _____ man who owned the slave in question 56.

58. _____ orator who testified against Paul in Caesarea.

59. _____ woman who reported the problems in Corinth to Paul.

60. _____ Timothy's grandmother.

61. _____ Timothy's mother.

62. _____ three rulers whom Paul appeared before.

63. _____ name three children of King Agrippa I.

64. _____ gospel writer who presented Christ as a man.

65. _____ gospel writer who presented Christ as God.

66. _____ gospel writer who presented Christ as a servant.

II. Identify the following places: (1 point each)

1. _____ city where the church started.

2. _____ where Jesus was baptized.

3. _____ city where people were first called Christians.

4. _____ city where Paul stayed two years.

5. _____ city where Paul stayed with friends and made tents.

6. _____ city where Jesus grew up.

7. _____ city where the church was having all kinds of problems.

8. _____ city where Dorcas was from.

9. _____ city where Cornelius was from.

10. _____ where Paul met with the Ephesians elders.

11. _____ city where Philip's daughters lived.

12. _____ city where Timothy lived.

13. _____ city where Paul preached until midnight.

14. _____ city where Mary, Martha, and Lazarus lived.

15. _____ city where Jesus went when He was twelve years old.

16. _____ city where there was an altar to an unknown god.

17. _____ city where John Mark turned back.

18. _____ place where John was exiled.

19. _____ island where Paul was shipwrecked.

20. _____ place where Paul wrote a letter to a group of churches.

III Name the book.

1. _____ gives the history of the early church.

2. _____ tells about the birth of Christ.

3. _____ books that tell of Jesus' death.

4. _____ book that lists the Hall of Faith.

5. _____ where there was a church with many problems.

6. _____ two books that tell about us being free from the old law.

7. _____ book that tells about the raising of Lazarus.

8. _____ four books written to individuals.

9. _____ books written by Jesus' half-brothers.

10. _____ book that tells about Paul being an apostle.

11. _____ book that talks about our growing in faith.

12. _____ book that tells about John's visions.

13. _____ four books with only one chapter.

14. _____ book that talks about joy and rejoicing.

15. _____ book about a slave.

IV. Pick 10 stories in the New Testament and give a lesson we can put in our lives from each: (2 pts. each)

Stories   **Lesson**

Answers to Questions

Chapter 1: Short-Answer

(1) Matthew, Luke, (2) all of them, (3) They wrote for different reasons and to different people, (4) John, (5) John, (6) See notes in chapter 1 (7) See notes in chapter 1, (8) John, (9) Matthew, Mark, Luke, John, Peter, Paul, James, Jude, (10) See notes, (11) Greek.

Thought Questions: Answers will vary.

Chapter 2: Short-Answer

(1) Greek, (2) Matthew and Luke, (3) John, (4) check answers in chapter one, (5) check in chapter one, (6) Ruth and Rahab, (7) Micah, (8) Isaiah, (9) Herod the Great, (10) Simeon and Anna,(11) Zacharias and Elizabeth , (12) His mother was old and barren, (13) Judah, (14) Matthew traces through Joseph and Luke traces through Mary, (15) 8th day, (16) two turtledoves, (17) Jordan, (18) camel's hair and a leather belt, ate locusts and wild honey. (19) Stones to bread, Jump off the temple, Bow down to Satan, (20) Galilee, Samaria, and Judea.

Thought Questions: Answers will vary.

Short-Answer: Who Am I?

(1) Matthew, (2) Peter, (3) Andrew, (4) Simon, (5) Nathaniel, (6) Peter, (7) Peter, Andrew, James, John, (8) Peter, Andrew, and James, John, (9)Thomas, (10) James, John, (11) Peter, (12) Judas, (13) Judas, (14) Simon the Zealot, (15) Peter, (16) Judas, (17) John, (18) James, (19) Mathias, (20) Peter, James, John, (21) John, (22) Thaddaeus, (23) Matthias, Paul, (24) Nathaniel, (25) James, John.

Thought Questions: Answers will vary.

Chapter 3: Short-Answer Review Questions

(1) Judea, Samaria, Judea, (2) Jordan River, (3) Bethlehem, (4) Nazareth, (5) 400 yrs., (6) roads (7) Hebrew to Greek, (8) refer to ch. 1, (9) prophecy, internal evidence, and doesn't conflict with science, (10) Paul, (11) Luke and Acts, (12) John, 1, 2, 3 John and Revelation (13) 39 in Old Testament and 27 in New Testament, (14) gospels, (15) history, (16) letters/epistles, (17) king, servant, man, God, (18) Jews, Romans, Greeks, Christians, (19) John, (20) Matthew, Luke, (21) all four, (22) Matt., Mark, Luke, John, Peter, Paul, James, Jude, (23) Greek, (24) Mediterranean Sea, (25) Micah, (26) Isaiah, (27) Don't know how many, (28) Herod the Great, (29) Ruth, Rahab, (30) Simeon, Anna, (31) Zacharias, Elizabeth, (32) Elizabeth while he was in the womb, (33) 6 months, (34) Judah, (35) stones to bread, jump from the temple, bow down to Satan, (36) Archelaus, (37) parables, question/answer, objects, one on one, (38) check Matthew 10:2-4 or this book, (39) in a house, (40) answers will vary.

Thought Questions: Answers will vary.

Chapter 4: Thought Questions: Answers will vary.

Chapter 5: Short-Answer

(1) Gethsemane, (2) Peter, James, John, (3) kiss, (4) Peter, Malchus, (5) Annas, (6) Caiaphas, (7) Peter, cock (rooster), (8) Death required the approval of the Romans, (9) Blasphemy, (10) Jesus was from Galilee, (11) hanged (12) Barabbas, (13) Nicodemus, (14) Simon.

Thought Questions: Answers will vary.

Matching (1) D, (2) A, (3) F, (4) C, (5) B, (6) E, (7) G, (8) I, (9) H, (10) J.

Chapter 6: Short-Answer

(1) Theophilus, (2) Luke, (3) Peter, John, (4) Gamaliel, (5) 3,000, (6) Barnabas, (7) 40 years, (8) Jerusalem, (9) 120, (10) Mt. Olivet, (11) 40 days, (12) See notes, (13) Acts 1-12: the early church; Acts 13-28: activities of Paul, (14) Peter: Jews; Paul: Gentiles, (15) Been

with Jesus, witness of His resurrection, (16) Will you restore the kingdom at this time? (17) Repent and be baptized, (18) Remission of sins, gift of the Holy Spirit.

Thought Questions: Answers will vary.

Chapter 7: Short-Answer

(1) Grecian widows, (2) 7, (3) Stephen and Phillip, (4) angry or upset, (5) stoned, (6) laid their clothes at Paul's feet when they were stoning Stephen, (7) "Lay not this sin to their charge," (8) Saul-prison, (9) Samaria, (10) Simon, buy, (11) repent and pray, (12) Ethiopian (eunuch), (13) worship (Jerusalem), (14) baptized, (15) Damascus, (16) bright light, to go into the city and it would be told him what to do, (17) Ananias, (18) "Arise and be baptized and wash away your sins, (19) Arabia, (20) Dorcas or Tabitha, (21) Joppa, (22) clothes, (23) Cornelius, Caesarea, (24) sheet with animals, rise, kill and eat, (25) friends, relatives, (26) Antioch, (27) James, Peter, (28) Peter, Mary's, (29) eaten of worms, (30) Rhoda, Peter.

Thought Questions: Answers will vary.

Matching: (1) G, (2) E, (3) I, (4) H, (5) A, (6) B, (7) J, (8) D, (9) F, (10) C.

Matching Review: (1) I, (2) L, (3) A, (4) H, (5) J, (6) E, (7) C, (8) K, (9) F, (10) B, (11) G, (12) D.

Chapter 8: Short-Answer

(1) Paul, Barnabas, John Mark, (2) Lydia and her household, (3) searched the Scriptures, (4) about an unknown God, (5) Aquila and Priscilla, (6) Apollos, (7) fell out the window, (8) prophet who predicted Paul's capture, (9) Tyrannus, (10) man asking him to come to Macedonia.

Name the Place: (1) Lystra, (2) Corinth, (3) Ephesus, (4) Antioch, (5) Island of Miletus, (6) Athens, (7) Troas, (8) Caesarea, (9) Lystra, (10) Philippi, (11) Jerusalem.

Thought Questions: Answers will vary.

Chapter 9: Short-Answer

(1) Told the officials that he was a Roman citizen, (2) 40, (3) Tertullus (4) 470, (5) troublemaker, profaned the temple, (6) Felix, Festus, (7) Julius, (8) northeaster, (9) Told Paul that he would go to Rome, (10) 276, (11) chief official, Paul healed his father, (12) 2 years.

Thought Questions: Answers will vary.

Chapter 10: Thought Questions: Answers will vary.

Chapter 11: Short-Answer

(1) churches and individuals, (2) Timothy, Titus, and Philemon, (3) Romans-God has paid our debt, 1 Corinthians-Problems in the church, 2 Corinthians-Paul as an apostle, Galatians-free from law, Ephesians-Building up the church, Philippians-rejoice, Colossians-Christ is above all (4) Paul, third journey, (5) see chapter, (6) Phoebe took the letter as she was going to Rome, (7) See chapter, (8) division, marriage, lawsuits, eating food, immorality (9) see Ephesians 6:10-18, (10) see Colossians 3:5-17, (11) see Philippians 4:8-9, (12) see Galatians 5:10-26, (13)) beatings, shipwreck, imprisonments, riots, see 2 Corinthians 6:3-10.

Chapter 12: Short-Answer: See notes in the chapter.

Thought Questions: Answers will vary.

Chapter 13: Use notes in the chapters.

Final Exam

I. Characters

1. Isaiah
2. Micah
3. Judah
4. Herod the Great
5. Simeon, Anna
6. Zacharias, Elizabeth
7. Matthew
8. Peter
9. James
10. Andrew
11. Peter, Andrew, James, John
12. Thomas
13. Matthias
14. James, John
15. John
16. John
17. Paul
18. Annas, Caiaphas
19. Mary Magdalene
20. Malchus
21. Herod Antipas
22. Herod Agrippa II
23. Nicodemus
24. Simon
25. Pilate
26. Luke
27. Theophilus
28. John Mark, Barnabas
29. Silas
30. Barnabas
31. Joel
32. Peter
33. Paul
34. Ananias, Sapphira
35. Ethiopian
36. Mary, mother of John Mark
37. Herod Agrippa I
38. Cornelius
39. Dorcas/Tabitha
40. Stephen
41. Philip
42. John Mark
43. Lydia
44. Jailor
45. Ananias
46. Simon
47. Demetrius
48. Aquila, Priscilla
49. Timothy, Titus
50. Agabus
51. Philip
52. Eutychus
53. Julius
54. Phoebe
55. Euodia, Syntyche
56. Onesimus
57. Philemon
58. Tertullus
59. Chloe
60. Lois
61. Eunice
62. Felix, Festus, Agrippa II
63. Agrippa II, Bernice, Drusilla
64. Luke
64. John
66. Mark

II. Places

1. Jerusalem	11. Caesarea
2. Jordan River	12. Lystra
3. Antioch	13. Troas
4. Ephesus	14. Bethany
5. Corinth	15. Jerusalem
6. Nazareth	16. Athens
7. Corinth	17. Perga
8. Joppa	18. Isle of Patmos
9. Caesarea	19. Malta
10. Miletus	20. Galatia

III. Name the Book

1. Acts	9. James, John
2. Matthew, Luke	10. 2 Corinthians
3. all four Gospels	11. Hebrews
4. Hebrews	12. Revelation
5. 1 Corinthians	13. Philemon, Jude, 2, 3 John
6. Galatians, Hebrews	14. Philippians
7. John	15. Philemon
8. 1, 2 Timothy, Titus, Philemon	

IV. Stories and lessons will vary.